T0219706

Develop Intelligent iOS Apps with Swift

Understand Texts, Classify Sentiments, and Autodetect Answers in Text Using NLP

Özgür Sahin

Apress®

Develop Intelligent iOS Apps with Swift: Understand Texts, Classify Sentiments, and Autodetect Answers in Text Using NLP

Özgür Sahin
Feneryolu Mh. Goztepe, Istanbul, Turkey

ISBN-13 (pbk): 978-1-4842-6420-1   ISBN-13 (electronic): 978-1-4842-6421-8
https://doi.org/10.1007/978-1-4842-6421-8

Copyright © 2021 by Özgür Sahin

Managing Director, Apress Media LLC: Welmoed Spahr
Acquisitions Editor: Aaron Black
Development Editor: James Markham
Coordinating Editor: Jessica Vakili

Distributed to the book trade worldwide by Springer Science+Business Media New York, 1 NY Plaza, New York, NY 10014. Phone 1-800-SPRINGER, fax (201) 348-4505, e-mail orders-ny@springer-sbm.com, or visit www.springeronline.com. Apress Media, LLC is a California LLC and the sole member (owner) is Springer Science + Business Media Finance Inc (SSBM Finance Inc). SSBM Finance Inc is a **Delaware** corporation.

For information on translations, please e-mail booktranslations@springernature.com; for reprint, paperback, or audio rights, please e-mail bookpermissions@springernature.com.

Apress titles may be purchased in bulk for academic, corporate, or promotional use. eBook versions and licenses are also available for most titles. For more information, reference our Print and eBook Bulk Sales web page at http://www.apress.com/bulk-sales.

Any source code or other supplementary material referenced by the author in this book is available to readers on GitHub via the book's product page, located at www.apress.com/978-1-4842-6420-1. For more detailed information, please visit http://www.apress.com/source-code.

Printed on acid-free paper

I would like to dedicate this book to my beautiful, cheerful, and beloved Evrim and take this opportunity to propose to her. Will you be my fellow in this life and marry me, my love? (^‿^)

—Özgür Şahin

Table of Contents

About the Author ix

About the Technical Reviewer xi

Acknowledgments xiii

Chapter 1: A Gentle Introduction to ML and NLP 1

What Is Machine Learning?..1

Supervised Learning 5

Unsupervised Learning 6

    Basic Terminology of ML 7

What Is Deep Learning? 10

What Is Natural Language Processing 12

Summary..15

Chapter 2: Introduction to Apple ML Tools 17

Vision 17

    Face and Body Detection..18

    Image Analysis 19

    Text Detection and Recognition 22

    Other Capabilities of Vision..25

VisionKit 26

Natural Language..27

    Language Identification 27

    Tokenization 28

Part-of-Speech Tagging 30

Identifying People, Places, and Organizations 31

NLEmbedding 33

Speech 35

Core ML 36

Create ML 37

Turi Create 38

Chapter 3: Text Classification 41

Spam Classification with the Create ML Framework 41

Train a Model in macOS Playgrounds 43

Spam Classification with the Create ML App 57

Spam Classification with Turi Create 62

Turi Create Setup 62

Training a Text Classifier with Turi Create 64

Summary 67

Chapter 4: Text Generation 69

GPT-2 69

Let's Build OCR and the Text Generator App 72

Using the Built-in OCR 74

Text Generation Using AI Model 78

Summary 85

Chapter 5: Finding Answers in a Text Document 87

BERT 87

Building a Question-Answering App 92

BERT-SQuAD 92

Examine the Core ML Model 93

Let's Build the App 97

Using the BERT Model in iOS 98

Building the UI of the App 105

Speech Recognition with the Speech Framework 112

Summary...118

Chapter 6: Text Summarization 121

What Is Text Summarization?..121

Building the Text Summarizer App 123

Summary...135

Chapter 7: Integrating Keras Models...............................137

Converting the Keras Model into Core ML Format 137

   Training the Text Classification Model in Keras 138

   Testing the Core ML Model 147

Testing the Core ML Model in Jupyter Notebook 149

Testing the Core ML Model in Xcode..154

   Using the Core ML Model in Xcode..157

Summary...164

Conclusion 164

Index...165

About the Author

Özgür Sahin has been developing iOS software since 2012. He holds a bachelor's degree in computer engineering and a master's in deep learning. Currently, he serves as CTO for Iceberg Tech, an AI solutions startup. He develops iOS apps focused on AR and Core ML using face recognition and demographic detection capabilities. He writes iOS machine learning tutorials for Fritz AI and also runs a local iOS machine learning mail group to teach iOS ML tools to Turkey. In his free time, Özgür develops deep learning–based iOS apps.

About the Technical Reviewer

Felipe Laso is Senior Systems Engineer at Lextech Global Services. He's also an aspiring game designer/programmer. You can follow him on Twitter at @iFeliLMor or on his blog.

Acknowledgments

I'd like to take this opportunity to gratefully thank the people who have contributed toward the development of this book:

Aaron Black, Senior Editor at Apress, who saw potential in the idea behind the book. He helped kick-start the book with his intuitive suggestions.

James Markham, Development Editor at Apress, who made sure that the content quality of the book remains uncompromised.

Jessica Vakili, Coordinating Editor at Apress, who made sure that the process from penning to publishing the book remained smooth and hassle-free.

Mom, Dad, and my love, Evrim, all of whom were nothing but supportive while I was writing this book. They have always been there for me, encouraging me to achieve my aspirations.

Countless number of iOS developers who share their knowledge with the community.

I hope many developers find this book guiding through their first steps to mobile machine learning (ML). You encourage me to learn more and share.

Thanks!

## CHAPTER 1

A Gentle Introduction to ML and NLP

This chapter will provide you a bird's-eye view of machine learning (ML) and deep learning (DL). The history of these fields will be storified here in order to be more understandable. We will examine why they have emerged and what kind of applications they have. After gaining the principal knowledge, you will be introduced to natural language processing (NLP). You will learn how we make text data understandable for computers via NLP. Even if you have zero knowledge about these disciplines, you will gain the intuition behind after reading this chapter.

What Is Machine Learning?

As *Homo sapiens*, we like to create tools that will save us time and energy. First, humans started to use animals to be freed of manpower. With the industrial revolution, we started to use machines instead of the human body. The current focus of humanity is to transfer thinking and learning skills to machines to get rid of mundane mental tasks. The improvement of this field in the last decades is very significant. We don't have general AI yet that can do any intellectual task, but we have built successful AI models that can do specific tasks very well like understanding human language or finding the answer to a question in an article. In some tasks like image classification, it is even better than humans.

© Özgür Sahin 2021
Ö. Sahin, *Develop Intelligent iOS Apps with Swift*,
https://doi.org/10.1007/978-1-4842-6421-8_1

Machine learning is a buzzword nowadays. There are plenty of theories going around, but it's hard to see real applications that can be built by an indie developer. Developing an end-to-end machine learning system requires a wide range of expertise in areas like linear algebra, vector calculus, statistics, and optimization.

Therefore, from a developer's perspective, there's a high learning curve that stands in the way, but the latest tools take care of most of the work for developers, leaving them free to code. In this book, you will learn how to build machine learning applications that can extract text from an image (OCR), classify text, find answers in an article, summarize text, and generate sentences when given an input sentence. You will be armed with cutting-edge tools offered by Apple and able to develop your smart apps. We will learn by coding; some of the apps we will develop will look like those in Figure 1-1.

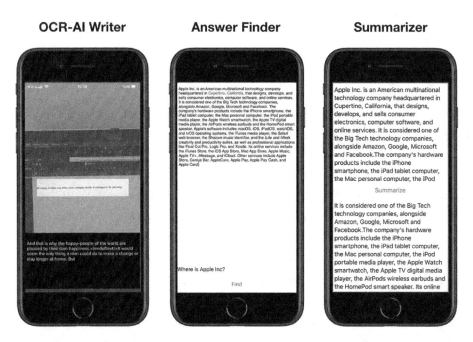

Figure 1-1. *Smart Apps*

Machine learning is an active field of research that studies how computer algorithms can learn from data without explicitly programming them.

What do we mean by without explicitly programming? Let's consider an example. One type of machine learning algorithms is the classification algorithm. Let's say we want to classify positive and negative emails. In normal programming, we would write some if-else to check if certain words exist in the mail as shown in Listing 1-1.

Listing 1-1. Code for Determining Email Positivity

```
if mail.contains("good") ||
mail.contains("fantastic") ||
mail.contains("elegant")

{ mailEmotion = "positive"}

else {mailEmotion = "negative"}
```

How could we solve the same problem using machine learning? We would find many samples of positive and negative emails and categorize them as positive and negative. We feed this data to our model, and the model optimizes its structure to fit the pattern in this data. Figure 1-2 shows sample data which has categorized emails.

Training Examples	Labels
Simply loved it	Positive
Most disgusting food I have ever had	Negative
Stay away, very disgusting food!	Negative
Menu is absolutely perfect, loved it!	Positive
A really good value for money	Positive
This is a very good restaurant	Positive
Terrible experience!	Negative
This place has best food	Positive
This place has most pathetic serving food!	Negative

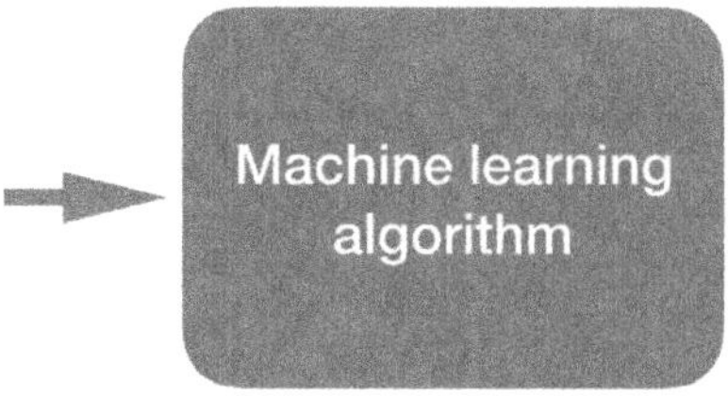

Machine learning algorithm

Figure 1-2. *Training ML Model*

3

By running many iterations, the model learns to separate these sentences without writing any specific code for this problem. It only learns by seeing many examples. After our model structure starts to predict many labels correctly, we save the model structure.

Now, we can use this saved model structure for new predictions. By giving it a sample email as an input, it will output whether the email is positive or negative as shown in Figure 1-3.

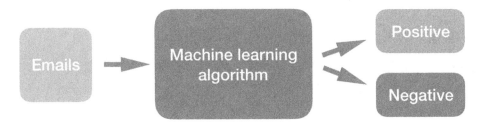

Figure 1-3. *Prediction Using ML Model*

Machine learning is often categorized into two categories: supervised learning and unsupervised learning.

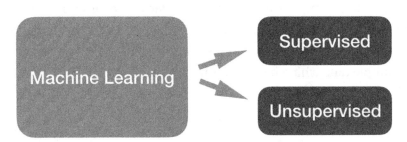

Figure 1-4. *Machine Learning Categories*

Supervised Learning

I find this example from Adam Geitgey very intuitive to understand supervised learning. Let's say you are a real estate agent and you glance at a house and predict its worth very precisely. You want to hire a trainee agent, but they don't have your experience so they can't predict the worth of a house precisely.

To help your trainee, you have noted some details like number of bedrooms, size, neighborhood, and the price for every house sale you've closed for the last 3 months. Table 1-1 shows the training data.

Table 1-1. *House sale records*

Bedrooms	Sq. Feet	Neighborhood	Price
3	2000	Normaltown	$250.000
3	800	Hipstertown	$300.000
2	850	Normaltown	$150.000
1	550	Normaltown	$78.000

Using this training data, we want to create a program that can estimate any other house in this area. Let say the house details shown in Table 1-2 are given, and we need to guess its price.

Table 1-2. *Prediction of the house price*

Bedrooms	Sq. Feet	Neighborhood	Price
3	2000	Hipstertown	???

This is called supervised learning. You have the records of the price (label) of each house sale in your area, so you know the answer of the problem. You could work backward and find some logic that affects the price.

Supervised learning is the machine learning type that learns with labeled examples like in these real estate records. It's similar to teaching a child by showing animals and calling their names. You teach it with classified examples.

The labels change according to data. For example, in sentiment analysis, we want to classify the emotion of a given text. These labels could be in the form as shown in Table 1-3.

Table 1-3. *Sample sentiment dataset*

Text	Label
I didn't like it.	Negative
This is a good book.	Positive

In this type of data, we know what our aim is (in this case the sentiment categories). There is a pattern between text and labels. We want to model this pattern mathematically by training a model on this data. After training, our model is ready to use to predict a text's sentiment; using its mathematical structure, it tries to mimic this function.

The label could be anything you can imagine: for an animal picture dataset, it could be the animal species; for a language translation dataset, the translated word; for a sound dataset, the sound type; for an auto-completion dataset, the next letter; and so on. Data can be in many forms: text, sound, images, and so on. Supervised learning is to learn by seeing this kind of data, like when the teacher teaches the kid by showing true and false.

Unsupervised Learning

In this type of learning, the data does not have a label column. So we let the machine learning model figure out the pattern or group in the data. Imagine you found many no-name old cassette tapes in an old box. You started listening to all of them until you gained some intuition to understand genre differences. With this intuition, you could classify them according to genre. This is unsupervised learning. You aren't offered classified tapes to learn as in the real estate agent example.

Let's consider another example. Let's say we have a dataset that consists of book reviews as seen in Table 1-4.

Table 1-4. *Sample text dataset*

Text	Gender	Age	Location	Year
This book is itself a work of genius.	Male	35	New York	2015
The physical quality of the book was very good.	Female	40	San Francisco	2014
I didn't like this book.	Female	30	Los Angeles	2019

This dataset is personal information about the buyer of the book. For this type of data, we may want to let the ML model cluster data. This clustering may unleash the hidden pattern in the data that we may not see with the naked eye.

For example, we may deduct that customers who are located in New York and female are more likely to be aged between 35 and 50. In this type of learning, we don't direct the ML model with a specific category label. Instead, the model figures out itself whether there is a higher-level relationship in the dataset.

Basic Terminology of ML

You will hear the concepts like training, testing, model, iteration, layer, and neural network a lot while developing ML applications. Let's cover what they are.

Machine learning focuses on developing algorithms that can learn patterns in a given set of input data. These algorithms are generally called a **model**. These models have mathematical structures that can change to fit the patterns in the input data. The data we use in the training period is called **training data**. We divide the input data into batches and run the model many times by feeding it with these batches. This is called **training**. Each run with a batch of the data is called **iteration** or **epoch**. In this training period, the model optimizes itself according to **the error function**. If the model fits the pattern in the input data and produces similar outputs, this error rate is lower; otherwise, it's higher. Training is stopped when the error rate is low enough, and we save this form of the model.

After training, we want to test how good our model has become. This is performed with **test data** which is put aside from input data and not used in training (e.g., 20% of the input data). So we test it on data that it has not seen before and see whether it has generalized the knowledge or just memorizes the training data. This data is called test data.

After testing the model and ensuring it works properly, we can run it with sample data and check its output; this is called prediction or inference. To sum up, we train the model using training data, evaluate the model using test data, save the model, and then make predictions using the trained model. Usual lifecycle of machine learning projects is like shown in Figure 1-5.

Figure 1-5. *Lifecycle of Machine Learning*

There are many types of machine learning algorithms like regression, decision tree, random forest, neural network, and so on. We will cover only neural networks here as they're also the basis of deep learning models.

A neural network is layers of interconnected neurons (nodes) that are designed to process information. Similar to neurons in the human brain, these mathematical neurons know how to take in inputs, apply weights to them, and calculate an output value. Until the mid-2000s, these neural networks used to have a couple of layers as shown in Figure 1-6 and were not able to learn complex patterns.

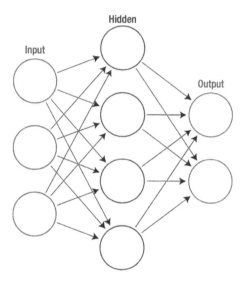

Figure 1-6. *Neural Network*

After that period, researchers found out that by using many layers of these neurons, we can model more complex functions like image classification. Models that have more than a couple of layers are called a deep neural network. Processing information with deep neural networks requires many matrix operations. Using the CPU of computers takes a long time to do this kind of operation. As GPUs can do this kind of operation in parallel, they can solve these problems faster. They are also more affordable nowadays, and many people are able to train deep neural networks with their PCs.

What Is Deep Learning?

In the last decades, thanks to artificial neural networks, we started to teach machines to recognize images, sound, and text. Using more layers of neural networks led us to teach more complex things to computers. This opened up a new field called deep learning that focuses on teaching with examples by using more layered networks as shown in Figure 1-7.

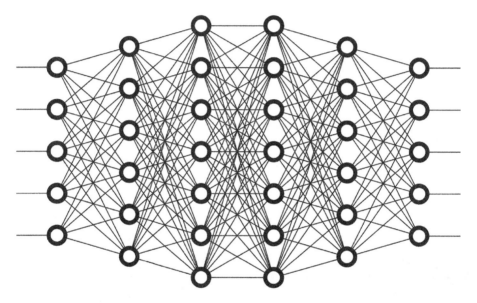

Figure 1-7. *Deep Neural Network*

Deep learning lets us develop many diverse applications that can recognize faces, detect noisy sounds, and classify text as positive and negative. Deep learning algorithms started to reform many fields.

Deep learning's rise started with the ImageNet moment. ILSVRC (ImageNet Large-Scale Visual Recognition Challenge) is a visual recognition challenge where applicants' algorithms compete to classify and detect objects in a large image dataset. This ImageNet dataset has more than 14 million labeled images categorized into 21841 classes. Figure 1-8 shows some samples from ImageNet dataset.

In 2012, a deep neural network called AlexNet had a significant score in this challenge. With the success of the AlexNet, all competitors started to use deep learning-based techniques in 2013. In 2015, these algorithms showed better performance than humans, by surpassing our image recognition level (95%). These advances made deep learning models more popular. These models started to appear in a variety of industries from language translation to manufacturing.

ImageNet Challenge

- 1,000 object classes (categories).
- Images:
  - 1.2 M train
  - 100k test.

Figure 1-8. *ImageNet Dataset*

We can't laugh at the translation of Google anymore as we did in the past after they switched to neural machine translation in 2016. This translation algorithm lets Google Translate to support 103 languages (used to be a few languages before), translating over 140 billion words every day. Autonomous cars were a future dream once; nowadays, they are on the roads. Siri understands your commands and acts on your behalf. Your mobile phone suggests words while writing your messages. We can produce faces that never existed before and even animate faces and imitate voices and create fake videos of celebrities. It also has applications

11

in the medical industry. It helps clinicians in classifying skin melanoma, ECG rhythm strip interpretation, and diabetic retinopathy images. Apple Watch can detect atrial fibrillation, a dangerous arrhythmia that can result in a stroke.

Deep learning has many applications as you see, and it increases day by day. In the last decade, deep learning has shown to be very effective both in computer vision and NLP.

What Is Natural Language Processing

Natural language processing (NLP) is a subset of artificial intelligence that focuses on interactions between computers and human languages.

The main objective of NLP is to analyze, understand, and process natural language data. Nowadays, most of the NLP tasks take advantage of machine learning to process text and derive meaning. With NLP techniques, we can create many useful tools that can detect the emotion (sentiment) of the text, find the author of a piece of writing, create chatbots, find answers in a document, and so on.

The applications of NLP are very common in our lives. Amazon Echo and Alexa, Google Translate, and Siri are the products that use natural language processing to understand textual data.

With the latest ML tools offered by Apple, you don't need a deep understanding of NLP to use it in your projects. For further understanding, more resources will be shared in this book.

Let's briefly take a look at how NLP works, how it has evolved, and where it is used.

Sebastian Ruder (research scientist at DeepMind) discusses major recent advances in NLP focusing on neural network–based methods in his review "A Review of the Neural History of Natural Language Processing." It's a recommended read if you have an entry-level understanding of machine learning. I will summarize the milestones in NLP briefly from his review.

Language modeling is predicting the next word according to the previous text. In 2001, the first neural language model that used a feed-forward neural network was proposed. Before this work, n-grams were popular among researchers. N-grams are basically a set of co-occurring words as shown in Table 1-5.

Table 1-5. *N-grams*

Sample	1-Gram	2-Gram
to be or not to be	to, be, or, not, to, be	to be, be or, or not, not to, to be

Another key term you will often hear in natural language processing is word embedding. Word embeddings have a long history in NLP. Word embedding is the mathematical representation of a word. For example, we can represent words in the text with the number of occurrences (frequency) of each word. This is called the bag-of-words model.

In 2013, Tomas Mikolov and his team made the training of these word embeddings more efficient and introduced word2vec, a two-layer neural network that processes text and outputs their vectors. This network is not a deep learning network, but it is useful for deep learning models as it creates computational data that can be processed by computers.

It is very practical as it represents words in a vector space as shown in Figure 1-9. This allows doing mathematical calculations on word vectors like adding, subtracting, and so on. Thanks to word2vec, we can deduce the relation between man and woman, king and queen. For instance, we can do this calculation: "King – Man + Woman = Queen."

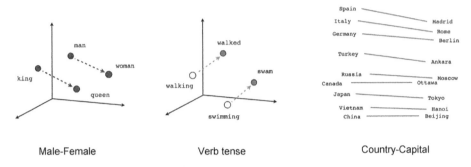

Male-Female   Verb tense   Country-Capital

Figure 1-9. *Relations captured by word2vec (Mikolov et al., 2013a, 2013b)*

With word2vec, we can deduce interesting relations; for example, we can ask "If Donald Trump is a Republican, what's Barack Obama ?," and word2vec will produce [Democratic, GOP, Democrats, McCain]. The data we give says Donald Trump is Republican, and we want to find similar relations for Barack Obama, and it says he is a Democrat. This kind of deduction offers limitless possibilities that you can derive from textual data.

After 2013, more deep learning models started to be used in NLP. Recurrent neural networks (RNNs) and long short-term memory (LSTM) networks became more popular.

In 2014, Ilya Sutskever proposed a sequence-to-sequence (Seq2Seq) learning framework that allows mapping one text to another using a neural network. This framework is proved to be very practical for machine translation. Google Translate started to use this framework in 2016 and replaced its phrase-based translation with deep LSTM network. According to Google's Jeff Dean, this resulted in replacing **500,000 lines** of phrase-based machine translation code with a **500-line** neural network model.

In 2018, pretrained language models showed a big step forward by showing improvements over state of the art. These models are trained on a large amount of unlabeled data (e.g., Wikipedia articles). This teaches model usage of various words and how language works in general. The model can transfer this knowledge to any specific task by using a smaller task-specific dataset. These models are like "well-read" people who are knowledgeable and can learn more easily than being ignorant.

2018 is the year of a big step in NLP with the occurrence of the new pretrained language models like ULMFit, ELMo, and OpenAI transformer.

Before these models, we needed a large amount of task-specific data to train natural language models. Now, with these knowledgeable models, we can train models on any language-specific task easily.

In the last chapter, we will develop a smart iOS application that can find answers of a question in a given text by using the BERT model.

Summary

In this chapter, the general concepts of machine learning, deep learning, and natural language processing have been introduced. We tried to understand the intuition behind deep learning and NLP by looking at how they are improved over the last decades. The next chapters will be more practical as we will use NLP techniques in iOS development and build smart applications.

## CHAPTER 2

Introduction to Apple ML Tools

In the software and machine learning world, it's very important to learn and try the latest tools. If you don't know how to use these productivity tools, you may waste a lot of time. This chapter will introduce the tools Apple provides to build ML applications easily for iOS developers. The frameworks and tools introduced in this chapter are Vision, VisionKit, Natural Language, Speech, Core ML, Create ML, and Turi Create. We will learn what capabilities these tools have to offer and what kind of applications we can build using them.

Vision

The Vision framework deals with images and videos. It offers a variety of computer vision and machine learning capabilities to apply to visual data. Some capabilities of the Vision framework include face detection, body detection, animal detection, text detection and recognition, barcode recognition, object tracking, image alignment, and so on. I will mention the main features and methods considering some hidden gems of iOS that you may not have heard of. As this book focuses on text processing, it won't cover the details of image processing. If you need more information related to computer vision algorithms, you can find the details and sample projects on the Apple Developer website.

© Özgür Sahin 2021
Ö. Sahin, *Develop Intelligent iOS Apps with Swift*,
https://doi.org/10.1007/978-1-4842-6421-8_2

Face and Body Detection

Vision has several request types for detecting faces and humans in images. I will mention some of the requests here to recall what Apple provides with built-in APIs. VNDetectFaceRectanglesRequest is used for face detection which returns the rectangles of faces detected in a given image yaw angle. It also provides a face's yaw and roll angles. VNDetectFaceLandmarksRequest gives you the location of the mouth, eyes, face contour, eyebrow, nose, and lips. VNDetectFaceCaptureQualityRequest captures the quality of the face in an image that you can use in selfie editing applications. There is a sample project, namely, "Selecting a Selfie Based on Capture Quality," which compares face qualities across images.

VNDetectHumanRectanglesRequest detects humans and returns the rectangles that locate humans in images.

To use these requests, you create an ImageRequestHandler and a specific type of request. Pass this request to the handler with the perform method as shown in Listing 2-1. This executes the request on an image buffer and returns the results. The sample shows face detection on a given image.

Listing 2-1. Face Detection Request

```
let handler = VNImageRequestHandler(cvPixelBuffer:
pixelBuffer, orientation: .leftMirrored, options:
requestOptions)

        let faceDetectionRequest =
VNDetectFaceCaptureQualityRequest()

        do {

            try
handler.perform([faceDetectionRequest])

            guard let faceObservations =
```

```
faceDetectionRequest.results as? [VNFaceObservation]
else {return}

            }

        } catch {

            print("Vision error: \
(error.localizedDescription)")

        }
```

Image Analysis

With the built-in image analysis capabilities, you can create applications that understand what is in the image. You can detect and locate rectangles, faces, barcodes, and text in images using the Vision framework. If you want to dig deeper, Apple offers a sample project where they show how to detect text and QR codes in images.

Apple also offers a built-in ML model that can classify 1303 classes. It has many classes from vehicles to animals and objects. Some examples are acrobat, airplane, biscuit, bear, bed, kitchen sink, tuna, volcano, zebra, and so on.

You can get the list of these classes by calling the knownClassifications method as shown in Listing 2-2.

Listing 2-2. Built-in Image Classes

```
let handler = VNImageRequestHandler(cgImage:
image.cgImage!, options: [:])

let classes = try VNClassifyImageRequest.knownClassifications(
forRevision:
VNDetectFaceLandmarksRequestRevision1)

let classIdentifiers = classes.map({$0.identifier})
```

I created a Swift playground showing how to use the built-in classifier.[1] Apple made it super-simple to classify images. The sample code in Listing 2-3 is all you need to classify images.

Listing 2-3. Image Classification

```
import Vision

let handler = VNImageRequestHandler(cgImage: image,
options: [:])

let request = VNClassifyImageRequest()

try? handler.perform([request])

let observations = request.results as?
[VNClassificationObservation]
```

Another capability of the Vision framework is image similarity detection. This can be achieved using VNGenerateImageFeaturePrintRequest. This creates the feature print of the image, and then you can compare this feature print using the computeDistance method. The code sample in Listing 2-4 shows how to use this method. Again, we create ImageRequestHandler and a request and then call perform to execute this request.

Listing 2-4. Create a Feature Print of an Image

```
func featureprintObservationForImage(atURL url: URL)
-> VNFeaturePrintObservation? {

    let requestHandler =
VNImageRequestHandler(url: url, options: [:])
```

---

[1]https://github.com/ozgurshn/Swift-Playgrounds-For-the-Book/tree/master/ClassifyImagewithBuiltinRequest.playground

```
    let request =
VNGenerateImageFeaturePrintRequest()

        do {

            try requestHandler.perform([request])

            return request.results?.first as?
VNFeaturePrintObservation

        } catch {

            print("Vision error: \(error)")

            return nil

        }

    }
```

This function creates a feature print of an image. It is a mathematical representation of an image which we can use to compare with other images. Listing 2-5 show how to use this feature print to compare images.

Listing 2-5. Feature Print

```
let apple1 = featureprintObservationForImage(atURL:
Bundle.main.url(forResource:"apple1", withExtension:
"jpg")!)

let apple2 = featureprintObservationForImage(atURL:
Bundle.main.url(forResource:"apple2", withExtension:
"jpg")!)

let pear = featureprintObservationForImage(atURL:
Bundle.main.url(forResource:"pear", withExtension:
"jpg")!)

var distance = Float(0)
```

```
try apple1!.computeDistance(&distance, to: apple2!)

var distance2 = Float(0)

try apple1!.computeDistance(&distance2, to: pear!)
```

Here, I am comparing pear to apple images. The image distance results are shown in Figure 2-1.

Figure 2-1. *Comparing Image Distances*

You can find the full code sample of the Swift playground in the link found in the corresponding footnote.[2]

Text Detection and Recognition

To detect and recognize text in images, you don't need any third-party framework. Apple offers these capabilities with the Vision framework.

You can use VNDetectTextRectanglesRequest to detect text areas in the image. It returns rectangular bounding boxes with origin and size.

---

[2]https://github.com/ozgurshn/Swift-Playgrounds-For-the-Book/tree/master/CompareImages.playground

If you want to detect each character box separately, you should set the reportCharacterBoxes variable to true.

The Vision framework also provides text recognition (optical character recognition) capability which you can use to process text from scanned documents or business cards.

Figure 2-2 shows the text recognition that runs on a playground.

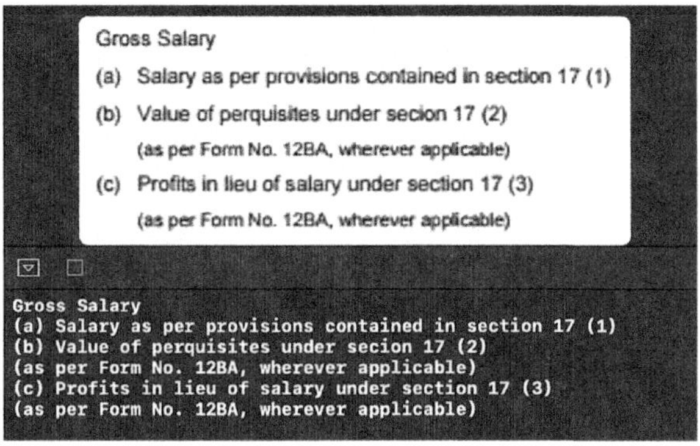

Figure 2-2. *Text Recognition Results*

Similar to other Vision functions, to process text in images, we create VNRecognizeTextRequest as shown in Listing 2-6 and perform this request using VNImageRequestHandler. Text request has a closure which is called when the process is finished. It returns the observations for each text rectangle it detects.

Listing 2-6. Text Recognition

```
let textRecognitionRequest = VNRecognizeTextRequest {
(request, error) in

    guard let observations = request.results as?
[VNRecognizedTextObservation] else {

        print("The observations are of an unexpected type.")
```

```swift
        return

    }

    let maximumCandidates = 1

    for observation in observations {

        guard let candidate =
observation.topCandidates(maximumCandidates).first
else { continue }

        textResults += candidate.string + "\n"

    }

}

    }

}

let requestHandler = VNImageRequestHandler(cgImage:
image, options: [:])

do {

    try
requestHandler.perform([textRecognitionRequest])

} catch {

    print(error)

}
```

Text recognition request has a recognitionLevel property which is used to trade off between accuracy and speed. You can set it accurate or fast.

Other Capabilities of Vision

The Vision framework provides other capabilities like image saliency analysis, horizon detection, and object recognition. With image saliency analysis, iOS lets us detect which parts of the image draw people's attention. It also offers object-based attention saliency which detects foreground objects. You can use these features to crop images automatically or generate heat maps. These two types of requests are VNGenerateAttentionBasedSaliencyImageRequest (attention based) and VNGenerateObjectnessBasedSaliencyImageRequest (object based). Similar to other Vision APIs, you create a request and perform it using the image request handler as shown in Listing 2-7.

Listing 2-7. Image Saliency

```
let request =
VNGenerateAttentionBasedSaliencyImageRequest()

try? requestHandler.perform([request])
```

Horizon detection lets us determine the horizon angle in the image. With this request (VNDetectHorizonRequest), you can get the image angle and the CGAffineTransform required to fix the image orientation. You can also use VNHomographicImageRegistrationRequest to determine the perspective warp matrix needed to align two images.

Another capability of Vision is object recognition. You can use the built-in VNClassifyImageRequest to detect objects, or you can create a custom model using Create ML or Turi Create if you want to train on your own image dataset.

VisionKit

If you ever used the Notes app on iOS, you might have used the built-in document scanner which is shown in Figure 2-3. VisionKit lets us use this powerful document scanner in our apps. Implementation is very simple:

1. Present the document camera as shown in Listing 2-8.

Listing 2-8. Instantiate Document Camera

```
let vc = VNDocumentCameraViewController()

vc.delegate = self

present(vc, animated: true)
```

2. Implement the VNDocumentCameraViewControllerDelegate to receive callbacks as shown in Listing 2-9. It returns an image of each page with the following function.

Listing 2-9. Capture Scanned Document Images

```
  func documentCameraViewController(_ controller:
VNDocumentCameraViewController, didFinishWith scan:
VNDocumentCameraScan) {

    var scannedImageList = []

    for pageNumber in 0 ..< scan.pageCount {

                              let image =
scan.imageOfPage(at: pageNumber)

self.scannedImageList.append(image)

                    }

}
```

Figure 2-3. *Built-in Document Scanner*

Natural Language

The Natural Language framework lets you analyze text data and extract knowledge. It provides functions like language identification, tokenization (enumerating words in a string), lemmatization, part-of-speech tagging, and named entity recognition.

Language Identification

Language identification lets you determine the language of the text. We can detect the language of a given text by using the NLLanguageRecognizer class. It supports 57 languages. Check the code in Listing 2-10 to detect the language of a given string.

27

Listing 2-10. Language Recognition

```
import NaturalLanguage

let recognizer = NLLanguageRecognizer()

recognizer.processString("hello")

let lang = recognizer.dominantLanguage
```

Tokenization

Before we can perform natural language processing on a text, we need to apply some preprocessing to make the data more understandable for computers. Usually, we need to split the words to process the text and remove any punctuation marks. Apple provides NLTokenizer to enumerate the words, so there's no need to manually parse spaces between words. Also, some languages like Chinese and Japanese don't use spaces to delimit words; luckily, NLTokenizer handles these edge cases for you. The code sample in Listing 2-11 shows how to enumerate words in a given string.

Listing 2-11. Enumerating Words

```
import NaturalLanguage

let text = "A colourful image of blood vessel cells
has won this year's Reflections of Research
competition, run by the British Heart Foundation"

let tokenizer = NLTokenizer(unit: .word)

tokenizer.string = text

tokenizer.enumerateTokens(in:
text.startIndex..<text.endIndex) { tokenRange, _ in
```

```
print(text[tokenRange])

return true
}
```

As you see, we import the NaturalLanguage framework and create NLTokenizer by specifying the unit type. This allows us to determine the enumeration type; here, we can enumerate documents, words, paragraphs, or sentences. The enumerateTokens function enumerates the selected token type (word, in this case) and returns closure for each word. In closure, we print each word enumerated, and the result is shown in Figure 2-4.

Figure 2-4. *Tokenization*

Part-of-Speech Tagging

To understand the language better, we need to identify the words and their functions in a given sentence. Part-of-speech tagging allows us to classify nouns, verbs, adjectives, and other parts of speech in a string. Apple provides a linguistic tagger that analyzes natural language text called NLTagger.

The code sample in Listing 2-12 shows how to detect the tags of the words by using NLTagger. Lexical class is a scheme that classifies tokens according to class: part of speech, type of punctuation, or whitespace. We use this scheme and print each word's type.

Listing 2-12. Word Tagging

```
import NaturalLanguage

let text = "The ripe taste of cheese improves with
age."

let tagger = NLTagger(tagSchemes: [.lexicalClass])

tagger.string = text

let options: NLTagger.Options =
[.omitPunctuation, .omitWhitespace]

tagger.enumerateTags(in:
text.startIndex..<text.endIndex, unit: .word, scheme:
.lexicalClass, options: options) { tag, tokenRange in

    if let tag = tag {

        print("\(text[tokenRange]):  \(tag.rawValue)")

    }

    return true

}
```

As you can see in Figure 2-5, it successfully determines the types of words.

Figure 2-5. *Determining Word Types*

When using NLTagger, depending on the type that you want to detect, you can specify one or more tag schemes (NLTagScheme) as a parameter. For example, the tokenType scheme classifies words, punctuations, and spaces; and the lexicalClass scheme classifies word types, punctuation types, and spaces.

While enumerating the tags, you can skip the specific types (e.g., by setting the options parameter). In the preceding code, the punctuations and spaces options are set to [.omitPunctuation, .omitWhitespace].

NLTagger can detect all of these lexical classes: noun, verb, adjective, adverb, pronoun, determiner, particle, preposition, number, conjunction, interjection, classifier, idiom, otherWord, sentenceTerminator, openQuote, closeQuote, openParenthesis, closeParenthesis, wordJoiner, dash, otherPunctuation, paragraphBreak, and otherWhitespace.

Identifying People, Places, and Organizations

NLTagger also makes it very easy to detect people's names, places, and organization names in a given text.

Finding this type of data in text-based apps opens new ways to deliver information to users. For example, you can create an app that

31

can automatically summarize the text by showing how many times these names (people, places, and organizations) are referred to in that text (via blog, news article, etc.).

Take a look to Listing 2-13 to see how we can detect these names in a sample sentence.

Listing 2-13. Identify People and Places

```
import NaturalLanguage

let text = "Prime Minister Boris Johnson has urged
the EU to re-open the withdrawal deal reached with
Theresa May, and to make key changes that would allow
it to be passed by Parliament."

let tagger = NLTagger(tagSchemes: [.nameType ])

tagger.string = text

let options: NLTagger.Options =

    [.omitPunctuation, .omitWhitespace, .joinNames]

let tags: [NLTag] =

[.personalName, .placeName, .organizationName, .adver
b ,NLTag.pronoun, NLTag.determiner, NLTag.noun ,

    NLTag.interjection ]

tagger.enumerateTags(in:

text.startIndex..<text.endIndex, unit: .word, scheme:

                        NLTagScheme.nameType,

options: options) { tag,

tokenRange in
```

```
if let tag = tag, tags.contains(tag) {

    print("\(text[tokenRange]):  \(tag.rawValue)")

    }

    return true

}
```

Here we use NLTagger again, but this time we set another option called joinNames, which concatenates names and surnames. To filter personal names, places, and organizations, we create an NLTag array.

The tags of the words that NLTagger can find are shown in Figure 2-6.

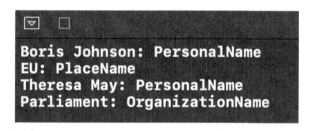

Figure 2-6. *Identifying People and Places*

As you can see, we can deduce specific knowledge from text using iOS's Natural Language framework.

NLEmbedding

Embedding in ML is used for mathematical representation of the given data. Here in Natural Language, it's used for vector representation of a word. After you convert the word to a vector, you can do arithmetic calculations on it. For example, you can calculate the distance between words or sum them up. Calculating the distance between words lets you find similar words.

NLEmbedding lets us determine the distance between two strings or find the nearest neighbors of a string in a word set. The higher the similarity of any two words, the smaller the distance between them. The code sample in Listing 2-14 shows how to calculate the distance between words.

Listing 2-14. Measuring Distance Between Words

```
import NaturalLanguage

//calculate distance between words

let embedding =
NLEmbedding.wordEmbedding(for:  .english)

let distance1 = embedding?.distance(between: "movie",
and: "film")

let distance2 = embedding?.distance(between: "movie",
and: "car")
```

In the preceding code, we use wordEmbedding and specify its language. Distance calculation is done using distance function. The distance between "movie" and "film" is 0.64 and between "movie" and "car" is 1.21. As you see, similar words have less distance between them. With this distance calculation, you can create apps that cluster words according to similarity or create recommendation apps that can detect similar texts or titles. You can even create custom embeddings for any kind of string. For example, you could make embeddings of news titles and recommend new articles based on the previous interest of your users. To create custom embeddings, you can use Create ML's MLWordEmbedding and export it as a file to use in your Xcode project. This will be covered later in the book after we learn Create ML.

Speech

The Speech framework provides speech recognition on live or prerecorded audio data. Using this framework, you can create transcriptions of spoken words in your apps. iOS built-in dictation support also uses speech recognition to convert audio data into text.

With this framework, you can create applications that understand verbal commands like Siri or Alexa. Apple says on-device speech recognition is available for some languages, but always assume that performing speech recognition requires network connection because this framework relies on Apple's servers for speech recognition.

To transcribe an audio, you should create a SFSpeechRecognizer instance for each language you want to support. Create SFSpeechRecognizer and SFSpeechAudioBufferRecognitionRequest to call the recognitionTask function which starts the speech recognition process and returns the result. Here we get the transcription results with result.bestTranscription. formattedString as seen in the code sample in Listing 2-15.

Listing 2-15. Speech Recognition

```
let recognitionRequest =
SFSpeechAudioBufferRecognitionRequest()

let recognitionTask =
speechRecognizer.recognitionTask(with:
recognitionRequest) { result, error in

    if let result = result {

        self.textView.text =
result.bestTranscription.formattedString

    }

}
```

If you want the result block to be called with partial transcription results, you can set recognitionRequest.shouldReportPartialResults to true.

Core ML

Apple announced the Core ML framework at WWDC 2017. This framework was Apple's alignment to the fast-developing machine learning world. Via Core ML, developers could integrate third-party machine learning models into their apps. Core ML APIs let us train and fine-tune ML models and make predictions, all on a user's device.

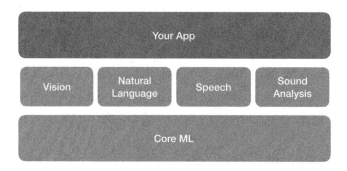

Figure 2-7. *Core ML*

As shown in Figure 2-7, Core ML is the underlying framework that powers Vision, Natural Language, Speech, and Sound Analysis frameworks.

A Python framework called coremltools was also made available to convert deep learning models from popular frameworks like Keras, Caffe, and scikit-learn to Core ML format.

To use coremltools, one needs to know Python. This created a learning barrier for iOS developers. To lower this barrier, Apple announced a simpler machine learning tool called Create ML in WWDC 2018.

Create ML

Create ML is a separate developer application like Xcode. It lets us create ML models easily, be it image classification, text classification, or sound classification. Thanks to this tool, iOS developers have fewer excuses for not developing smart iOS apps right now. Create ML and Xcode provide an end-to-end machine learning solution so developers can create their solutions all in Apple's ecosystem.

Create ML makes it easy to train models with image, text, or sound datasets and then test those models. When you finish training and testing, you can drag and drop your trained model from Create ML into your Xcode project.

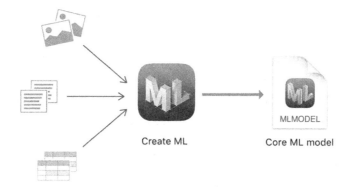

Create ML   Core ML model

Figure 2-8. *Create ML*

Create ML has ready-to-use templates to make training custom models easier. These templates include image classifier, object detector, sound classifier, activity classifier (motion classifier), text classifier, word tagger, tabular regressor, tabular classifier, and recommender. You can use Create ML as a separate application or as a framework in Swift Playgrounds.

Turi Create

To simplify the process of ML model training for developers, many decisions are done behind the scenes in Create ML. ML models have parameters that you can fine-tune to achieve better accuracy. If you are not satisfied with the choices Create ML offers and want more freedom over your ML models, you can use Turi Create.

In August 2016, Apple acquired Turi, a machine learning software startup, and open sourced and developed its library Turi Create. Turi Create is a Python framework that simplifies the development of custom machine learning models. You can export models from Turi Create for use in iOS, macOS, watchOS, and tvOS apps.

It supports a variety of data types: text, image, audio, video, and sensor data. You can create many different types of custom ML models using Turi Create. Some of them are text classification, image classification, object detection, regression (prediction of numeric values), clustering, activity classification, style transfer, and so on.

For text classification, it offers some preprocessing methods to clean the text data before training. For example, you can remove some words that have a small frequency or remove common words, for example, "and," "the," and so on (generally called stop words in the ML world).

When we say text classification, often sentiment analysis comes to people's minds, but there are many use cases. For instance, you can train a model on App Store app reviews and categorize the reviews as a feature request, complaint, compliment, and so on. Or you can determine the author of a piece of writing by training a model with writings. Anything you can imagine and have enough text samples of, you can train a classifier.

Another text processing capability of Turi Create is text analysis which lets us understand a large collection of documents. We can create "topic models" which are statistical models for text data. They represent documents with a small set of topics and can create a probability of any word to occur in a given "topic." This way we can represent large documents with five to ten words or find words that likely occur together. We will learn how to use Turi Create to train text classification models or to create topic models in the next chapters.

In this chapter, we covered the tools and frameworks Apple provides for ML. We looked at how to use the Vision framework to recognize text, VisionKit to scan documents, Natural Language to understand a text, Core ML and Create ML to train custom models, and finally Turi Create to train models with more advanced techniques. In the next chapters, we will dive deeper and create intelligent applications using Natural Language.

CHAPTER 3

Text Classification

Text classification is a natural language processing method that lets us categorize texts into predefined classes. This is a very popular technique that has a variety of use cases. One of the famous uses is classifying text into emotional categories (positive, negative, etc.) which is called sentiment analysis. This method can be used on any text data that has been categorized. Text classification allows us to find the author of a piece of writing, classify GitHub issues, find complaints in App Store reviews, or detect the language of a text. In this chapter, we will learn how to use Create ML and Turi Create to create text classification applications. We will learn by doing example apps. We will develop a spam SMS classifier app with Create ML first and then with Turi Create.

Spam Classification with the Create ML Framework

Apple uses *natural language processing techniques* in many ways on iOS. Thanks to NLP, iOS can auto-fix typos, and Siri can understand what we're saying. At WWDC 2018, Apple brought these capabilities to developers via a tool called Create ML. This tool has enabled developers to easily create text classification models (among numerous other kinds of models). Create ML became available in Swift Playgrounds with macOS 10.14.

© Özgür Sahin 2021
Ö. Sahin, *Develop Intelligent iOS Apps with Swift*,
https://doi.org/10.1007/978-1-4842-6421-8_3

To create a classification model with Create ML, the only thing we need is the labeled text data. This opens many doors for developers. We can detect the author of an article, find a company's best- and worst-reviewed products, and even detect various entities (person names, locations, organizations, etc.) in a given text. This is only limited by your imagination and data gathering techniques. In other words, the sky is the limit.

In this section, we'll dive into these frameworks to train a machine learning model in Create ML and develop a spam SMS classifier app as shown in Figure 3-1.

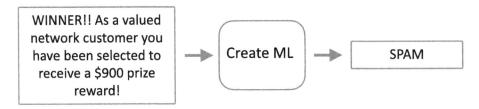

Figure 3-1. *Text Classification with Create ML*

We can use Create ML in two ways: as a separate app that can be opened in the Xcode menu bar by choosing "Open Developer Tool" and as a framework in macOS Playgrounds. In Playgrounds, we can import data from CSV/JSON files or folders into the Create ML app. Data should be categorized into folders. So in Playgrounds, we have more options.

In this project, we will use the SMS Spam Collection dataset on Kaggle. Kaggle is a great source to find datasets.

Download the SMS Spam Collection dataset from `www.kaggle.com/uciml/sms-spam-collection-dataset` to start the project. It's a simple CSV file with two columns as shown in Figure 3-2. The first column is the label of the SMS, and the second column is the SMS. We have two categories: ham and spam. It contains one set of 5,574 SMS messages in English, tagged according to being ham (legitimate) or spam.

v1	v2
ham	Go until jurong point, crazy.. Available only in bugis n great world la e buffet... Cine there got amore wat...
ham	Ok lar... Joking wif u oni...
spam	Free entry in 2 a wkly comp to win FA Cup final tkts 21st May 2005. Text FA to 87121 to receive entry question(std txt rate)T&C's apply 08452810075over18's
ham	U dun say so early hor... U c already then say...
ham	Nah I don't think he goes to usf, he lives around here though
spam	FreeMsg Hey there darling it's been 3 week's now and no word back! I'd like some fun you up for it still? Tb ok! XxX std chgs to send, £1.50 to rcv
ham	Even my brother is not like to speak with me. They treat me like aids patent.
ham	As per your request 'Melle Melle (Oru Minnaminunginte Nurungu Vettam)' has been set as your callertune for all Callers. Press *9 to copy your friends Callertune
spam	WINNER!! As a valued network customer you have been selected to receivea £900 prize reward! To claim call 09061701461. Claim code KL341. Valid 12 hour
spam	Had your mobile 11 months or more? U R entitled to Update to the latest colour mobiles with camera for Free! Call The Mobile Update Co FREE on 08002986C

Figure 3-2. *SMS Spam Collection Dataset*

Train a Model in macOS Playgrounds

Open Xcode and create a blank **macOS playground** as shown in Figure 3-3.

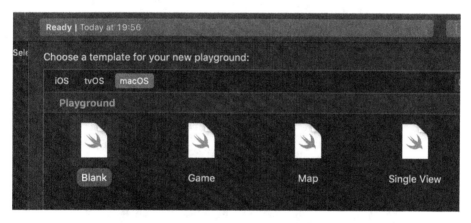

Figure 3-3. *Templates in Playgrounds*

Import the necessary frameworks (CreateML and Foundation) as shown in Figure 3-4.

43

Figure 3-4. *Importing in Playgrounds*

If you get an error saying CreateML is not available, ensure you selected macOS as platform in Playground Settings as shown in Figure 3-5.

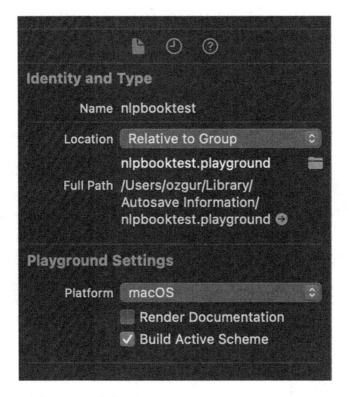

Figure 3-5. *Playground Settings*

After downloading the text file, pass the file path as a parameter to the URL object. Instead of writing this code, you can just drag and drop the file into Playgrounds to create the file path.

Create ML can read data in two ways: using folders as labels when files are separated in folders or reading from a single file (CSV, JSON).

First, we need to read the CSV file as MLDataTable. MLDataTable is a structure in Create ML that simplifies the loading and processing of text and tabular data. Most of the built-in machine learning models (MLTextClassfier, MLRegressor, MLClassifier, etc.) in Create ML read the data in MLDataTable format, so in order to train these models, we need to convert our raw training data to this format.

Listing 3-1. Create URL Object

```
let datasetURL = URL(fileURLWithPath: "/Users/ozgur/Desktop/
dataset/spam.csv")

var table = try MLDataTable(contentsOf: datasetURL)
```

In the preceding code, we create a URL object to point to the CSV file and pass that as a parameter to the MLDataTable.

Tip   You can drag and drop the CSV file into Playgrounds if you don't want to write it manually. It will create the file path.

You can also guide MLDataTable to use parsingOptions as in Listing 3-2, but this is not needed as we cleaned our dataset manually. With these options, we can guide parsing with settings like the delimiter and end-of-line character (lineTerminator) or whether our data contains a header (containsHeader). We can even choose the columns that we want to parse by setting the column names to the selectColumns parameter.

Listing 3-2. Parsing Options

```
let parsingOptions =
MLDataTable.ParsingOptions(containsHeader: true,
delimiter: ",", comment: "", escape: "\\",
doubleQuote: true, quote: "\"", skipInitialSpaces:
true, missingValues: ["NA"], lineTerminator: "\n",
selectColumns: ["v1","v2"], maxRows: nil, skipRows: 0)

var table2 = try MLDataTable(contentsOf:
datasetURL,options: parsingOptions)
```

Next, we create a model using MLTextClassifier to classify natural language text. We guide the MLTextClassifier by specifying the text column and the label column (spam or ham).

Listing 3-3. Training a Text Classifier

```
let classifier = try MLTextClassifier(trainingData:
table, textColumn: "v2", labelColumn: "v1")
```

Since our column names are "v1" and "v2," we specified them as shown in the preceding code. This model learns to associate labels with features of the input text, which can be sentences, paragraphs, or even entire documents.

Apple provides a model trainer called MLTextClassifier. It supports 57 languages. The model works in a supervised way, which means your training data needs to be labeled (in this case, the SMS text and the spam category of the text).

The model starts training when you run Create ML by clicking the play button as shown in Figure 3-6.

```
1
2  import CreateML
3  import Foundation
4  let datasetURL = URL(fileURLWithPath: "/Users/ozgur/Desktop/NLP book REFS/dataset/spam.csv")
5  var table = try MLDataTable(contentsOf: datasetURL)
6
   let classifier = try MLTextClassifier(trainingData: table, textColumn: "v2", labelColumn: "v1")
```

Figure 3-6. *Training the Text Classifier with MLTextClassifier*

During training, it will parse the text data, tokenize the text, and extract features. If you try to train this model, the error shown in Figure 3-7 is printed to the console.

```
65 lines failed to parse correctly
Finished parsing file /Users/ozgur/Desktop/NLP book REFS/dataset/spam.csv
Parsing completed. Parsed 2905 lines in 0.011777 secs.
Tokenizing data and extracting features
Playground execution terminated: An error was thrown and was not caught:
▿ Unknown internal error occurred.
  ▿ generic : 1 element
    - reason : "Unknown internal error occurred."
```

Figure 3-7. *Training Result with Error*

The error is not descriptive, but the problem is some of the punctuation that exists in our training data.

To solve this problem, just open the CSV file in TextEdit or some other text application and clean these punctuation marks: \, /, and " (replace all with an empty string).

The file has five columns; we will only use the first two columns. Open the CSV file in Numbers and remove the last three columns.

After cleaning the text, run again. You should see the following message in Figure 3-8.

```
Finished parsing file /Users/ozgur/Desktop/NLP book REFS/dataset/spamCleaned.csv
Parsing completed. Parsed 4286 lines in 0.0166 secs.
Tokenizing data and extracting features
10% complete
20% complete
30% complete
40% complete
50% complete
60% complete
70% complete
80% complete
90% complete
100% complete
Starting MaxEnt training with 4286 samples
Iteration 1 training accuracy 0.881241
Iteration 2 training accuracy 0.954970
Iteration 3 training accuracy 0.990201
Iteration 4 training accuracy 0.999300
Finished MaxEnt training in 0.09 seconds
```

Figure 3-8. *Training Output in the Console*

The duration can differ on different Macs, but on my MacBook Pro 2015, it just takes 0.09 second to train this model.

A better way to train the model is to split our data into train and test sets. This way we can evaluate the trained model and see how good it is on data it has not been trained on.

The code in Listing 3-4 splits data into trainingData (0.8) and testData (0.2) with the ratio of 0.8.

Listing 3-4. Training with Split Data

```
let (trainingData, testingData) =
table.randomSplit(by: 0.8)

let spamClassifier = try
MLTextClassifier(trainingData: trainingData,

                                    textColumn:
"v2",

labelColumn: "v1")
```

After training the classifier, you can check the training metrics by calling trainingMetrics as shown in Listing 3-5. It shows the accuracy of the model as shown in Figure 3-9.

Listing 3-5. Check Training Metrics

```
spamClassifier.trainingMetrics
```

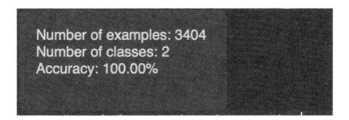

Figure 3-9. *Training Accuracy*

To evaluate the model on testing data, run the code in Listing 3-6. It shows how good the model is on data it has not seen before. This shows the actual success of the model. Figure 3-10 shows the evaluation metrics.

Listing 3-6. Evaluating the Model

```
let evaluationMetrics = spamClassifier.evaluation(on:
testingData, textColumn: "v2", labelColumn: "v1")
```

```
let evaluationMetrics = spamClassifier.evaluation(on: testingData, textColumn: "v2", labelColumn: "v1")

Number of examples: 882
Number of classes: 2
Accuracy: 97.28%
```

Figure 3-10. *Evaluate the Model*

Here we see that our model's accuracy is %97 on the testing data. It shows that our model is working well and not just memorizes the training data but also generalizes knowledge because it is also successful on the testing data.

You can also test your trained model with arbitrary text in Playgrounds.

Listing 3-7. Prediction Using the Model

```
try spamClassifier.prediction(from: "We are trying to
contact you. Last weekends draw shows that you won a
£1000 prize GUARANTEED. Call 09064012160.")
```

```
//spam
```

```
try spamClassifier.prediction(from: "We are trying to
contact you. Have you arrived to your house?")
```

```
//ham
```

Here we run our spam classifier model with some sentences, and it correctly categorizes this text.

If this model works for us, then we can save it and use it in an iOS app. To provide the model details, we create model metadata. This explanation is shown in Xcode when we open the model.

Listing 3-8. Export the Core ML Model

```
let metadata = MLModelMetadata(author: "Ozgur Sahin",
shortDescription: "Spam Classifier", license: "MIT",
version: "1.0")
```

```
try? classifier.write(to: URL(fileURLWithPath:
"users/ozgur/Desktop/SpamClassifier.mlmodel"))
```

We save the model by giving the path to the write function. Don't forget to set the path according to your folder structure. Core ML model files are saved with the mlmodel extension, so we set the file name as SpamClassifier.mlmodel.

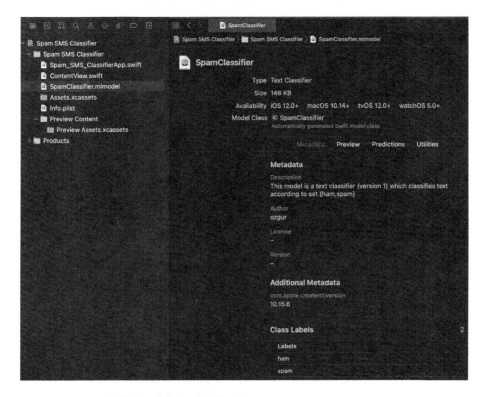

Figure 3-11. *MLModel in the Project*

Since we've exported our model, we're now ready to use it in an iOS app. Open Xcode and create a new project with App template. Make sure the interface is SwiftUI and lifecycle is SwiftUI app. After you created the project, drag and drop your Core ML model into the project.

You can also use Storyboard as a user interface, but here I will use SwiftUI because it's easier to show results there.

Click the model and check its details. The model is only 148 kb as you can see in Figure 3-11.

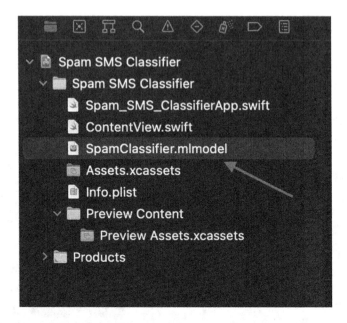

Figure 3-12. *Model Details*

In Xcode, we examine the model details and the metadata that we provided while exporting the model. It also shows the input and output types of the model.

When we drag and drop the model into the project, Xcode **automatically** creates a class for the model as shown in Figure 3-13. If you want to see the created code, click the class icon in Figure 3-13.

Figure 3-13. *SpamClassifier class generated by Xcode*

The class is shown in Figure 3-14. This class has the functions needed to load the model and make predictions.

Note   This class should not be edited.

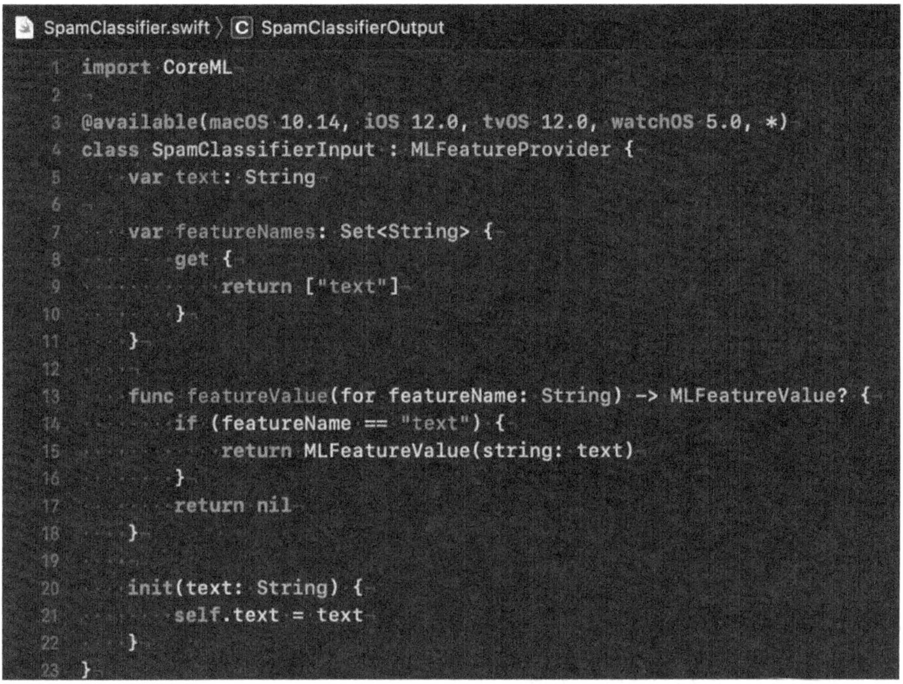

```
 SpamClassifier.swift ⟩ C  SpamClassifierOutput
 1  import CoreML
 2
 3  @available(macOS 10.14, iOS 12.0, tvOS 12.0, watchOS 5.0, *)
 4  class SpamClassifierInput : MLFeatureProvider {
 5      var text: String
 6
 7      var featureNames: Set<String> {
 8          get {
 9              return ["text"]
10          }
11      }
12
13      func featureValue(for featureName: String) -> MLFeatureValue? {
14          if (featureName == "text") {
15              return MLFeatureValue(string: text)
16          }
17          return nil
18      }
19
20      init(text: String) {
21          self.text = text
22      }
23  }
```

Figure 3-14. *Model's Auto-generated Class Code*

I created a class called Classifier and a simple function to use the model.

Listing 3-9. Using the Classifier Model in the Project

```
class Classifier
{
    static let shared = Classifier()
    func predict(text:String)->String?
```

```
{

    let spamClassifier = try?
SpamClassifier(configuration: MLModelConfiguration())

    let result = try?
spamClassifier?.prediction(text: text)

    return result?.label

  }

}
```

As shown in the preceding code, I created the model's instance and called a prediction on it. Prediction can throw an error; that's why we need to call it with a try. Ideally, you may wrap it in a do-catch block and handle the error.

In the ContentView of the project, add the code in Listing 3-10 to call the prediction method that we created before.

Listing 3-10. Calling Classifier in SwiftUI

```
@State var textInput:String = ""

  @State var classificationResult:String?

  var body: some View {

    VStack{

        Text("Spam SMS
Classifier!").font(.title).foregroundColor(.blue)

        Spacer()

        TextField("Enter SMS Message", text:
$textInput).multilineTextAlignment(.center).font(.tit
```

```
le).textFieldStyle(RoundedBorderTextFieldStyle())

        Button(action: {

            self.classificationResult =
Classifier.shared.predict(text: self.textInput)

        }) {

            Text("Classify").font(.title)

        }.frame(width:120,
height:40).foregroundColor(.white).background(Color.b
lue).cornerRadius(10)

        Text("Result:\(classificationResult ??
"")").foregroundColor(.red).font(.title)

        Spacer()

    }

}
```

In the preceding code, we created a text field and a button. When the user taps the button, we get the input from the text field and send it to our spam classifier model. The model's classification result is shown in the second text field.

After adding the code, you can just run the app by clicking the play button.

Figure 3-15. *Running the Spam SMS Classifier App*

This runs the application in SwiftUI preview as shown in Figure 3-15. Here, you can use your app like a simulator and test your spam classifier. Write some text in the text field and tap the Classify button to try out your smart application. Some samples are shown in Figure 3-16.

Figure 3-16. *Spam SMS Classifier App*

Congratulations! You just created a smart application that can detect spam SMS messages.

Spam Classification with the Create ML App

We trained the text classification model using the Create ML framework. Now, we will use the Create ML app (v1.0) to train the same model. Create ML has several project templates for a different type of data (image, text, sound). For this project, select the text classifier as shown in Figure 3-17.

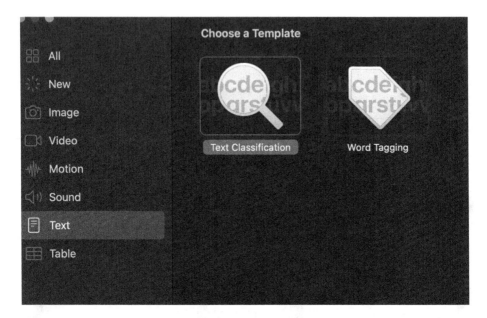

Figure 3-17. *Text Classifier Template in the Create ML App*

First, we need to provide training data. The text classifier in Create ML v1 only accepts text data in folders. Version 1.1 of Create ML is still in beta, and it will support reading from CSV and JSON files.

For v1, we need to parse our CSV file and create a text file for each row in the "ham" or "spam" folder. I wrote a simple function to parse the CSV and create files.

Listing 3-11. Read CSV and Create Text Files

```
import Cocoa

import CreateML

let datasetURL = URL(fileURLWithPath: "/Users/ozgur/
Desktop/NLP book REFS/dataset/spamCleaned.csv")

var table = try MLDataTable(contentsOf: datasetURL)
```

```swift
func createFiles(from rows:MLDataTable.Rows) {

    for (index,row) in rows.enumerated() {

        if let text = row["v2"]?.debugDescription,

            let label = row["v1"]?.debugDescription

        {

            do {

                var folder = "spam"

                if label == "ham"

                {

                    folder = "ham"

                }

                let fileURL = URL(fileURLWithPath: "/
Users/ozgur/Desktop/NLP book REFS/dataset/
spamsetInFolders/\(folder)/\(index).csv")

                try text.write(to: fileURL,
atomically: true, encoding: .utf8)

            } catch {

                print("error creating file")

            }

        }

    }

}

createFiles(from: table.rows)
```

You can change the file paths according to your computer and run this code in macOS Playgrounds. It will create the text files as shown in Figure 3-18.

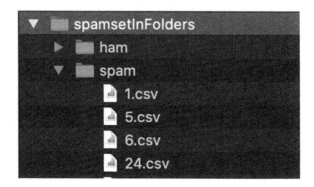

Figure 3-18.   *Text Files for the Create ML App*

Now we can drag and drop the parent folder ("spamsetInFolders") into the Training Data panel in the Create ML app. Alternatively, you can also select a folder in Finder by clicking Select Files in the Training Data panel.

Figure 3-19.   *Create ML App Training Data Panel*

The Create ML app will read the files and show the number of classes and file count. Create ML also offers some different algorithms to train your text classification model. Currently, the provided algorithms are maximum entropy, conditional random field, and transfer learning. In transfer learning, there are two options: static and dynamic embedding. Static embedding uses static vector representation for words and does not care about the context of the word. Dynamic embedding cares about the context of the word. So it creates separate vectors for the word "food" for these two samples: "food for thought" and "I need food." Static embedding, on the other hand, would create the same vectors.

Select your algorithm and click the Train button to start training the text classifier model. Create ML shows your current training status and accuracy over each iteration in a simple graph as shown in Figure 3-20.

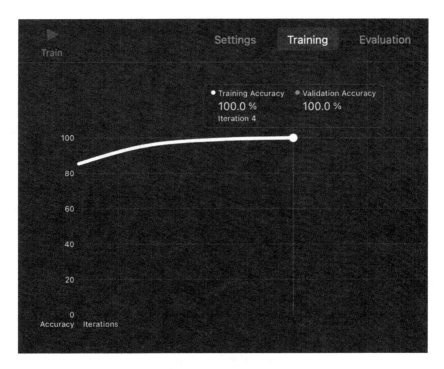

Figure 3-20. *Training in the Create ML App*

You can check the results of training and validation by clicking the tabs. For validation, Create ML puts a small percentage of training data aside to use for validating the model's progress. This improves the model's performance on examples the model hasn't been trained on. Validation accuracy lets Create ML understand when to stop training. Validation data split is done randomly, so you may see different results in each training.

If you have test data, you can test your model in the Testing tab. It's important to see how your model works on data it hasn't seen before. You can also test your model with the arbitrary text you enter in the Output tab. If you are satisfied with your model's accuracy, just drag and drop your model from the Output panel to a folder or Xcode project. You just trained your first model with the Create ML app. It's ready to use in your project.

Spam Classification with Turi Create

In the previous sections, we learned how to use the Create ML framework and Create ML app by creating a spam classifier in each one of them. In this section, we will train the spam classifier using Turi Create. Turi Create is an open source Python library for creating Core ML models. It supports a variety of tasks such as image classification, object detection, style transfer, recommendation, text classification, and more. Turi Create offers more parameters to train ML models compared to Create ML.

As this is a Python library, we cannot directly start coding; we have to set up our Python environment to start working with Turi Create.

Turi Create Setup

Turi Create supports Python versions 2.7, 3.5, 3.6, and 3.7. When dealing with Python projects, it is recommended to have a virtual environment. It simply keeps dependencies required by different projects separate by creating isolated Python virtual environments for them. The code in Listing 3-12 installs the virtualenv package and creates your virtual environment. Run in the terminal and activate your environment.

Listing 3-12. Create a Virtual Environment

```
pip install virtualenv

# Create a Python virtual environment

cd ~

virtualenv venv

# Activate your virtual environment source ~/venv/bin/activate
```

After activating the environment, install Turi Create using the code in Listing 3-13. You should see venv at the beginning of the line in the terminal if you are in your environment. Install Turi Create and iPython using the code in Listing 3-13. iPython lets us use interactive Python notebooks.

Listing 3-13. Install Turi Create and iPython

```
pip install -U turicreate

pip install ipython

ipython notebook
```

This code will open Jupyter on your browser. Click New and create a Python notebook. In the notebook, you can run the cells and see the results immediately. It is useful to make experiments and see the results in an interactive way.

Training a Text Classifier with Turi Create

Check the code in Listing 3-14 to see how easy it is to train a model in Turi Create.

Listing 3-14. Training the Spam Classifier with Turi Create

```
import turicreate as tc

# Read CSV

data = tc.SFrame.read_csv('/Users/ozgur/Desktop/
dataset/spamCleaned.csv', header=True, delimiter=',',
quote_char='\0')

# Rename the columns

data = data.rename({'v1': 'label', 'v2': 'text'})

# Split the data

training_data, test_data = data.random_split(0.8)

# Create a text classifier model

model = tc.text_classifier.create(training_data,
'label', features=['text'], max_iterations=100)

# Evaluate the model

metrics = model.evaluate(test_data)

print(metrics['accuracy'])

# Export for use in Core ML

model.export_coreml('SpamClassifierWithTuri.mlmodel')
```

With this code, we read the CSV file and rename columns as *label* and *text* for clarification. We split data into training (80%) and testing (20%). We create a text classifier model with 100 iterations; the default iteration count is 10. This lets more passes through data and can result in a more accurately trained model. Here, we can also specify **drop_stop_words** to ignore very common words like "the," "a," and "is" **word_count_threshold** to ignore less frequent words or **method** to use bag-of-words or bow logistic (logistic classifier). After training the model, we evaluate it using the test data. This shows how accurate the model is on data it hasn't seen. Finally, we export our Core ML model to use in the Xcode project.

Now, open the MLModel file you exported to see model details as shown in Figure 3-21. Its input is different than the models we trained with Create ML.

This model takes a bag-of-words representation of the text. Bag-of-words shows the number of times the words occurred in the text.

Name	Type	Description
▼ Prediction		
▼ Inputs		
text	Dictionary (String → Double)	
▼ Outputs		
label	String	
labelProbability	Dictionary (String → Double)	

Figure 3-21. *Spam Classifier Trained with Turi Create*

To create a bag-of-words representation of a text, we can use NSLinguisticTagger. The code in Listing 3-15 is taken from Apple's sample code in the Turi Create documentation.

Listing 3-15. Bag-of-Words Representation

```swift
func bow(text: String) -> [String: Double] {

    var bagOfWords = [String: Double]()

    let tagger = NSLinguisticTagger(tagSchemes:
[.tokenType], options: 0)

    let range = NSRange(location: 0, length:
text.utf16.count)

    let options: NSLinguisticTagger.Options =
[.omitPunctuation, .omitWhitespace]

    tagger.string = text.lowercased()

    tagger.enumerateTags(in: range, unit: .word,
scheme: .tokenType, options: options) { _,
tokenRange, _ in

        let word = (text as NSString).substring(with:
tokenRange)

        if bagOfWords[word] != nil {

            bagOfWords[word]! += 1

        } else {

            bagOfWords[word] = 1

        }

    }

    return bagOfWords

}
```

```
let bagOfWords = bow(text: text)

let prediction = try?
SpamClassifierWithTuri().prediction(text: bagOfWords)
```

In the preceding code, the "bow" function takes a string and returns a dictionary. The dictionary shows how many times each word occurs in the given text. Before using the model we exported from Turi Create, we create a bag-of-words representation of the text and give this to the model as an input.

Summary

In this chapter, we got our hands dirty by writing a spam SMS classifier app that can detect spam messages automatically. We learned how to use Apple's ML tools. By training a text classifier model in the Create ML framework, the Create ML app, and Turi Create, we learned their advantages and disadvantages. This chapter is intended to make you comfortable with these tools. In the next chapters, more complicated models will be trained to build more smart applications.

CHAPTER 4

Text Generation

Text generation lets us auto-complete the sentences with appropriate words or phrases. In recent years, text generation with neural network models significantly improved. These models often benefited from recurrent neural networks or transformers. In this chapter, we will learn how to use one of the best text generation models (GPT-2) and build an iOS application using this model. Our application will use built-in OCR capabilities to capture text from camera and generate text based on scanned sentences.

GPT-2

GPT-2 is a successor model to GPT (Generative Pretrained Transformer) published by OpenAI (AI research and deployment company based in San Francisco). The transformer is the architecture behind this model and many other language models. A transformer mainly consists of encoders and decoders. It also has attention layers that let the model focus on the specific parts of the input sequence. We won't go into much detail of the transformer as it's out of this book's context. Shallow knowledge is enough if you will just develop a mobile app using this model.

The original GPT-2 model is trained on 40 GB of Internet text (GPT-2 WebText). GPT-2 is a large transformer-based language model with 1.5 billion parameters, trained on a dataset. Language models train for predicting the next word given the previous words.

© Özgür Sahin 2021
Ö. Sahin, *Develop Intelligent iOS Apps with Swift*,
https://doi.org/10.1007/978-1-4842-6421-8_4

OpenAI didn't share their trained model due to their concerns about malicious applications of the technology. They shared a smaller version of this model for researchers to experiment with. Its completion works very well and sometimes produces amazing results. You can try this model with an arbitrary text input on this website: `https://transformer.huggingface.co/doc/gpt2-large`. The image in Figure 4-1 shows the prediction results given the sentence.

Figure 4-1. *GPT-2 Text Prediction*

To use this kind of model in iOS, you need to convert it to Core ML model format (models with a .mlmodel file extension). Conversion of this model is usually done with the coremltools library. This Python package is developed by Apple and supports conversion from TensorFlow and PyTorch.

Sometimes, the conversion of this model could be problematic, if there is a layer in the model which is not supported by coremltools. Luckily, Hugging Face open sourced their model implementation, conversion scripts, and even Core ML models. Hugging Face is a NLP-focused company, and they are famous with their open source framework transformers which have more than 30,000 stars on GitHub. They have a separate repo (swift-coreml-transformers) for transformer models converted to Core ML format to run on iOS devices. Currently, it contains GPT-2, DistilGPT-2, BERT (Bidirectional Encoder Representations from Transformers), and DistilBERT models. Models that start with "Distil" are models that are compressed. They are often faster and have fewer parameters. For example, DistilBERT has 40% fewer parameters than bert-base-uncased and runs 60% faster while preserving 97% of BERT's performances according to the GLUE benchmark.

We will use the DistilGPT-2 model to have predictions faster on mobile. If you are curious about the code to convert DistilGPT-2 to Core ML format, check out the code at `https://github.com/huggingface/swift-coreml-transformers/blob/master/model_generation/gpt2.py`. We will use the converted model in our sample project. The converted model can be downloaded from here: `https://github.com/huggingface/swift-coreml-transformers/blob/master/Resources/distilgpt2-64-6.mlmodel`.

The app we will develop will scan the texts from the camera and recognize them using built-in OCR. The result will be printed in the lower text view. If the user is satisfied with the recognized text, they will tap the scan area rectangle in the center, and it will start prediction with this text.

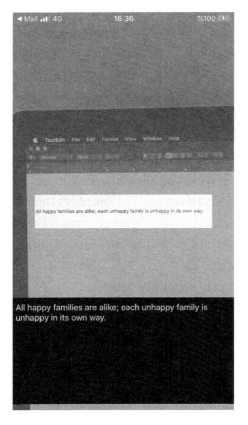

Figure 4-2. *OCR App*

We will discover how AI will continue if it writes after a famous quote in *Anna Karenina*.

> *All happy families are alike; each unhappy family is unhappy in its own way.*

—Leo Tolstoy

Let's Build OCR and the Text Generator App

Firstly, we will build the OCR functionality of the app. It will scan the camera stream and focus on the region of interest as seen in Figure 4-2. Scanning a smaller area lets us use our computational resources economically.

For the scanning part, we will use Apple's sample project "Reading Phone Numbers in Real Time" (`https://developer.apple.com/documentation/vision/reading_phone_numbers_in_real_time`) as a base project. It shows the best practices to process live capture and recognize the text in a focused area.

Download the starter project from here: `https://github.com/ozgurshn/Chapter3-ScanAndGenerate/tree/master/starter`. This is a template project that we set up for you to make things easier. You can also find the completed project here: `https://github.com/ozgurshn/Chapter3-ScanAndGenerate/tree/master/final`. I recommend starting with the starter project and following the exercises to understand implementation.

Let's open and check our starter project.

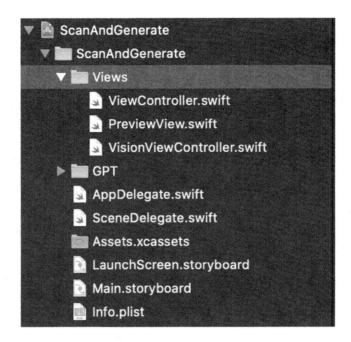

Figure 4-3. *Starter OCR and Text Generation Project*

Our sample project has Views and GPT folders as shown in Figure 4-3. Views contains ViewController-related files. GPT contains text generation–related classes. To focus you on specific tasks, many mundane tasks like camera setup and view positioning are done on your behalf. You only need to take care of OCR and text generation parts. We will develop it together using a starter project as a baseline.

Firstly, let's download the Core ML model for GPT-2 from `https://github.com/huggingface/swift-coreml-transformers/blob/master/Resources/distilgpt2-64-6.mlmodel` and drag and drop it into the GPT folder in the Xcode project.

The starter project has one view controller, namely, ViewController. swift; and VisionViewController is an extension of this view controller focusing only on Vision framework–related tasks (e.g., text recognition). PreviewView manages the video preview layer to show the camera stream properly.

The code parts where you need to write the implementation are marked with "TODO" as shown n Figure 4-4. Just click VisionViewController and check the to-do list.

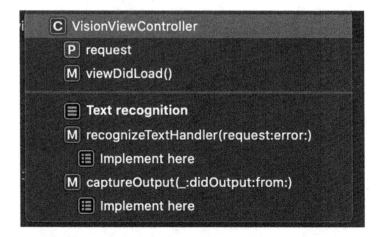

Figure 4-4. *VisionViewController Functions*

Using the Built-in OCR

Find the captureOutput function in VisionViewController; this function is called every time the camera captures a frame. Inside this function, we will process this frame and perform text recognition on it. Copy the code in Listing 4-1 into the "captureOutput" function.

Listing 4-1. Perform Text Recognition Request

```
        if let pixelBuffer =
CMSampleBufferGetImageBuffer(sampleBuffer) {

                // Configure for running in real-time.

                request.recognitionLevel = .fast

                request.usesLanguageCorrection = true
```

```
            // Only run on the region of
interest for maximum speed.

            request.regionOfInterest = regionOfInterest

            let requestHandler =
VNImageRequestHandler(cvPixelBuffer: pixelBuffer,
orientation: textOrientation, options: [:])
            do {

                try
requestHandler.perform([request])

            } catch {

                print(error)

            }

        }
```

With the preceding code, we create CVPixelBuffer from the sample buffer. Vision requests prefer the CVPixelBuffer type instead of CMPixelBuffer. VNRecognizeTextRequest is created in the viewDidLoad function; this prevents recreating it with every frame capture. VNRecognizeTextRequest has two options for recognition level: accurate or fast. We make this trade-off and choose fast to be more real time–friendly. Another property of this request is "usesLanguageCorrection"; this applies language recognition during the text recognition process. For maximum speed, we specify "regionOfInterest" to guide the recognition process on where to focus on the frame. Similar to all Vision requests, we create an image request handler with a pixel buffer and orientation and perform the Vision request.

We write the part that performs the text recognition request on captured frames. Next, we write the part that handles text recognition results.

Find the "recognizeTextHandler" function in the same file. This function is called after each text recognition process finishes. It's set in the "viewDidLoad" function while creating the Vision request. Copy the code in Listing 4-2 into the "recognizeTextHandler" function.

Listing 4-2. Text Recognition Process Results

```
        guard let results = request.results as?
[VNRecognizedTextObservation] else {

            return

    }

    let maximumCandidates = 1

  if let visionResult = results.first {

          guard let candidate =
visionResult.topCandidates(maximumCandidates).first
else { return }

      print(candidate.string)

      showString(string: candidate.string)

    }
```

In the preceding code, we check whether results exist in the request, and if they exist, we get the first result. This is the prediction result of the text recognition request. The "topCandidates" function returns the prediction results sorted by decreasing confidence score, so the top one is the best prediction. We get the prediction string for the first candidate and show it on the screen. The "showString" method takes the string and shows it in the text view. It dispatches this call in the main thread by calling DispatchQueue.main.async to ensure UI updates performed properly.

Our OCR app is ready. Now you can just run the app and try on your iPhone. If you focus the camera on any text, you will see the OCR results like in Figure 4-5. You can't use the simulator for this app because it does not provide camera capture.

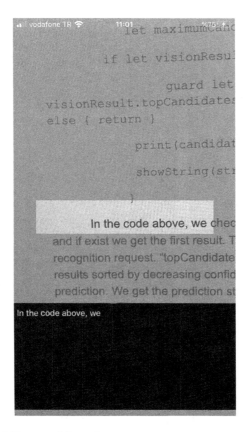

Figure 4-5. *Text Recognition App*

Now that we took care of the text recognition part, we will continue to build our app to generate text using the AI model.

Text Generation Using AI Model

In this part, we will integrate the text generation model (DistilGPT-2) into our project. The starter project already has the files you need as shown in Figure 4-6. Open the GPT folder and have a look at these files. The first file you see in this folder is the Core ML model version of DistilGPT-2. We will use this model to generate text based on input.

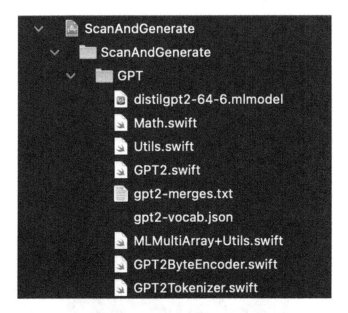

Figure 4-6. *GPT Files in the Project*

Let's examine this model by selecting it in Xcode. The first tab, namely, "Metadata," as seen in Figure 4-7, shows the metadata of the model like name, type, and size. The second tab, namely, "Predictions," shows the input and output types of the model. The last tab, namely, "Utilities," provides some functions for model encryption or hosting the model on CloudKit.

The model name is distilgpt2_64_6. The 64 in the model name stands for the sequence length (number of tokens) the model takes as an input.

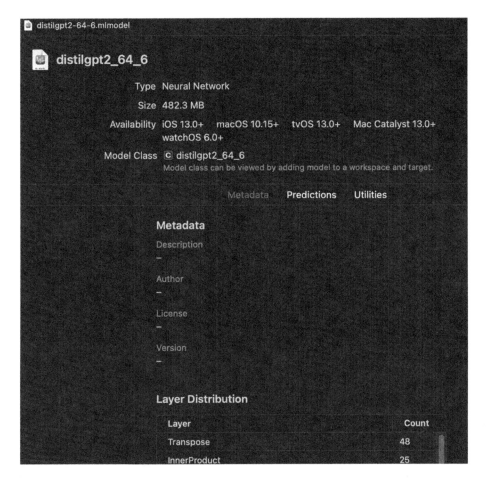

Figure 4-7. *DistilGPT-2 Model in Xcode*

The middle section on this screen shows the auto-generated Swift file that Xcode generates. The lower section shows the input and output types of the model. We need to convert the input text to model input format. As seen in the preceding image, the model takes two MultiArray that have 64 double values.

Luckily, the code to convert from text to model input format has been written by Julien Chaumond of Hugging Face. The files under the GPT folder are taken from their repo. Open the GPT2.swift file to check this code.

It has three decoding strategies: greedy (at each time step, the most likely next token is selected), topK (sample only from the top k most probable tokens), and topP (top tokens with a cumulative probability above a threshold). These decoding strategies determine how the prediction result is selected.

The prediction is done using the "predict" function in this class which is shown in Listing 4-3. This function predicts the next token from an array of previous tokens using the DistilGPT-2 model. Tokens are presented as corresponding numbers as mapped in the GPT2ByteEncoder.swift file. As AI models work better on numbers rather than texts, we convert text data to numbers.

Listing 4-3. Text Prediction Function

```swift
func predict(tokens: [Int]) -> Int {

    let maxTokens = (tokens.count > seqLen)

        ? Array(tokens[..<seqLen])

        : tokens
    /// Pad input_ids on the right, up to
`seqLen`:

    let input_ids = MLMultiArray.from(

        maxTokens + Array(repeating: 0, count:
seqLen - maxTokens.count)

    )

    let position_ids = MLMultiArray.from(

        Array(0..<seqLen)

    )
```

```
    let output = try! model.prediction(input_ids: input_ids,
position_ids:
position_ids)

    let outputLogits = MLMultiArray.slice(

        output.output_logits,

        indexing:
[.select(0), .select(maxTokens.count
- 1), .slice, .select(0), .select(0)]

        )

        switch strategy {

        case .greedy:

            let nextToken = Math.argmax(outputLogits)

            return nextToken.0

        case .topK(let k):

            let logits =
MLMultiArray.toDoubleArray(outputLogits)

            let topk = Math.topK(arr: logits, k: k)

            let sampleIndex = Math.sample(indexes:
topk.indexes, probs: topk.probs)

            return sampleIndex

        case .topP(_):

            fatalError("topP is not implemented yet")

        }
    }
```

The other function in this class is the "generate" function which is shown in Listing 4-4. It takes the text and the number of tokens to generate as an input. It encodes the input text and calls the prediction function with the input text and returns the results of the prediction. It appends each prediction result to the input tokens to make a prediction on the latest version of the text.

Lastly, it decodes the results to present in a text format instead of numbers.

Listing 4-4. Text Generation Function

```
func generate(text: String, nTokens: Int = 10,
callback: ((String, Double) -> Void)?) -> String {
        var tokens = tokenizer.encode(text: text)

        var newTokens: [Int] = []

        for i in 0..<nTokens {

            let (nextToken, time) = Utils.time {

                return predict(tokens: tokens)

            }

            tokens.append(nextToken)

            newTokens.append(nextToken)
print("🦄 <\(time)s>", i, nextToken,
tokens.count)

            callback?(

            tokenizer.decode(tokens: newTokens),
time)

        }
```

```
    return tokenizer.decode(tokens: newTokens)

}
```

We implemented the necessary functions to use the DistilGPT-2 model. Now, all we need is call the "generate" function when the user taps the cutout rectangle on the screen. To implement this function, find the "handleTap" method in the ViewController.swift file. Implement this function and the "generateText" function as shown in Listing 4-5.

Listing 4-5. Handling Tap Gesture

```
    @IBAction func handleTap(_ sender:
UITapGestureRecognizer) {

        captureSessionQueue.async {

            self.captureSession.stopRunning()

            self.generateText(input:
self.recognizedText)

        }

    }

    func generateText(input:String)

    {

DispatchQueue.global(qos: .userInitiated).async {

            _ = self.gpt2Model.generate(text: input,
nTokens: 50) { completion, time in
```

```
            DispatchQueue.main.async {

                self.textView.text = completion

            }

        }

    }

}
```

In the "handleTap" function, we stop capturing the camera session and call the generateText function with the recognized text.

In the "generateText" function, we call the "generate" function of gpt2Model with 50 tokens and present the generated text in the text view. We perform the UI updates in the main thread.

Congratulations! You just built a smart app that can recognize text and complete the recognized text using the AI model. Now, let's run the app on a device and see how it will complete *Anna Karenina*'s famous sentence. My model's result is as shown in Figure 4-8.

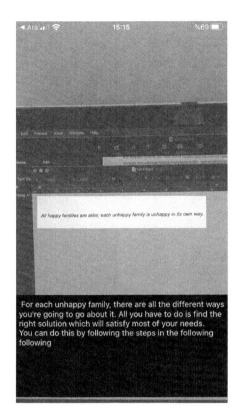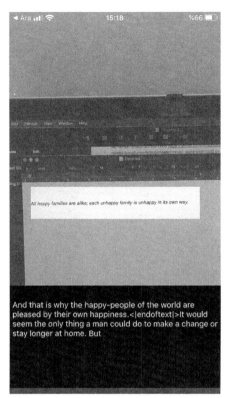

Figure 4-8. *AI Model Completing the Quote from Anne Karenina*

Summary

In this chapter, we learned how to use built-in text recognition capabilities of the Vision framework to build an OCR app that can read text from the phone's camera. We also used one of the best text generation models (DistilGPT-2) to generate sentences based on the recognized text.

## CHAPTER 5

Finding Answers in a Text Document

Have you ever wanted to find the answer by looking at a paper? Nowadays, we can do that using the latest AI model. NLP techniques are improved drastically over the last years. With the latest transformer models, we can even find answers to questions in a text document. In this chapter, we will learn how to develop an iOS app that is powered with this technology. The smart application will be able to find and highlight the answer in a given document and also speak the answer using text-to-speech. You will be introduced to the state-of-the-art NLP model of 2018 called BERT. A question-answering app will be developed to learn how to use this model in iOS.

BERT

BERT (Bidirectional Encoder Representations from Transformers) was published by researchers at Google AI Language in late 2018. It obtained new state-of-the-art results on eleven natural language processing tasks including question answering, named entity recognition, and other tasks related to general language understanding.

BERT's principal innovation is the bidirectional training of the transformer. Many previous models including GPT use left-to-right architecture where every token can only attend to previous tokens. In contrast, the BERT model reads input sequence at once, not sequentially

Ö. Sahin, *Develop Intelligent iOS Apps with Swift*,
https://doi.org/10.1007/978-1-4842-6421-8_5

from left to right; and it allows us to take into account not only previous tokens but also the next ones. The BERT model showed bidirectional training allows a deeper sense of the word context compared to unidirectional models.

During the training, the BERT model uses two training strategies: Masked LM and Next Sentence Prediction (NSP).

Masked LM is the technique performed by masking 15% of the words in each sequence randomly and enforcing a model to predict them. This allows the model to learn how to use information from the entire sentence in deducing missing words.

During the training process, the model is also enforced to guess the next sentence based on the previous sentence. The input for this task is 50% subsequent sentence pairs and 50% unrelated sentences. By training with this data, the model learns to predict the next sentence given the previous one.

The BERT model's architecture is based on the transformer. It consists of encoder layers. Since BERT's objective is to generate a language model, it only uses encoders. This chapter presents two architectures, BERT Base and BERT Large. The base model is sized as the OpenAI transformer to be comparable in performance. The large model is the bigger model that achieves state-of-the-art results. The base version has 12 encoder layers; the large version has 24 layers as shown in Figure 5-1.

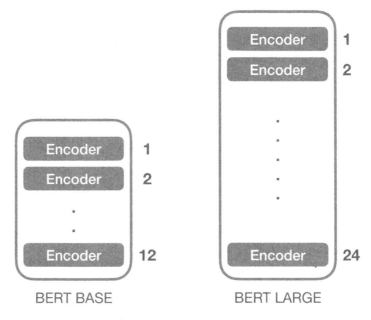

Figure 5-1. *BERT Model Architectures*

Unlike word2vec, the BERT model creates a vector representation of words based on the surrounding context of the words. It gets a deeper sense of the context in which the word is used.

The BERT model's knowledge can easily be transferred to a variety of NLP tasks (transfer learning). This makes it very useful. You can append a small layer specific to your use case. For example, you can add a classification layer to use it for classification as shown in Figure 5-2, or you can mark the beginning and the end of the answers and train a model for question answering.

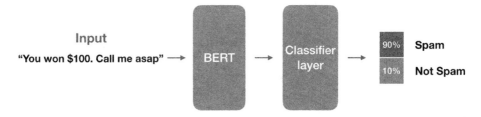

Figure 5-2. *Using BERT as a Classifier*

As mentioned earlier, one of the BERT training strategies is Next Sentence Prediction. Given a pair of sentences, it predicts if the second sentence is the actual next sentence of the first sentence. It can be used for question answering as it builds an understanding of the relationship between two sentences.

BERT uses a special token to understand the beginning of the input sequence ([CLS]), it separates sentences with a token ([SEP]), and it masks words randomly with a token ([MASK]).

By adding a single layer, we can fine-tune a model for Next Sentence Prediction as shown in Figure 5-3. Before feeding the data to the model, we tokenize the input text and use tokens to guide the model. Given to sentences separated with the [SEP] token, it can predict whether the next sentence is the actual next sentence of the first sentence.

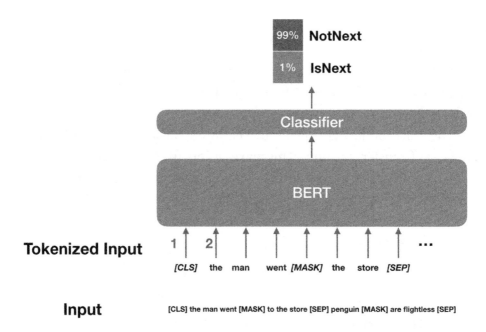

Figure 5-3. *Next Sentence Prediction*

Question answering is also framed as a prediction task. We give the model a question and a context paragraph, and the model predicts a start and an end token in the paragraph that most likely answers the question as shown in Figure 5-4. You guide the model with tokens that show what information you need in the text, and it's fine-tuned for that specific task, in this case, for question answering.

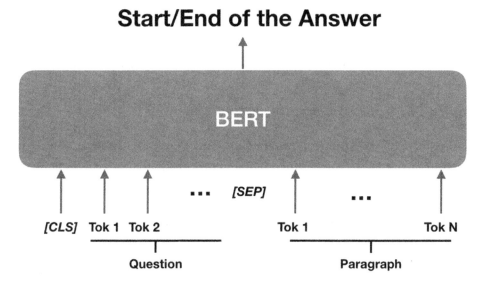

Figure 5-4. *Question Answering using BERT*

Demonstration with sentences and words may help you understand better. The sample text in Figure 5-5 is from a WWDC 2019 slide. We feed the fine-tuned model with a tokenized question and paragraph, and it locates the answer in the paragraph.

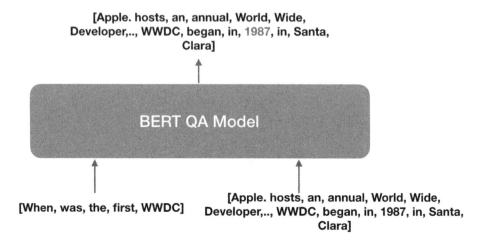

Figure 5-5. *BERT Question-Answering Model*

We have learned the working mechanism of the BERT model. Now, we will build a question-answering app using this model.

Building a Question-Answering App

We will build an app with SwiftUI that has two text views. One is for the paragraph and the other one for the question. The user will copy the paragraph, write the question, and tap a button. We will find the answer using the BERT question-answering model in the given text and highlight it for the user. Let's build the app and learn by doing.

BERT-SQuAD

SQuAd (Stanford Question Answering Dataset) is a dataset of questions on Wikipedia articles where the answer to every question is also included. SQuAD 2.0 has 100,000 answerable questions and 50,000 unanswerable questions. This helps machine learning models not only find the answers but also detect if there is not an answer in the given text.

The BERT-SQuAD model was fine-tuned to question answering using this dataset. It knows how to locate the answers in response to questions. Luckily, Apple published this model in Core ML format on their website (`https://ml-assets.apple.com/coreml/models/Text/QuestionAnswering/BERT_SQUAD/BERTSQUADFP16.mlmodel`). Download the BERT-SQuAD model from this link. The model's name is BERTSQUADFP16.mlmodel. FP16 means that the model weights are stored using half-precision (16-bit) floating-point numbers. This compresses the model into a smaller size.

Examine the Core ML Model

Open the model with Xcode to examine the model. This way we can see the inputs, output, size, and details like license, source of the model as shown in Figure 5-6. The Model class shows the auto-generated class of the model. This class is generated by Xcode to use the model.

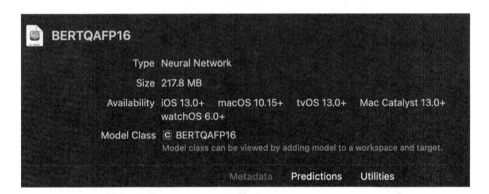

Figure 5-6. *BERTQA Model Metadata in Xcode*

The Metadata section in Xcode shows the general data about the model like the description, author, and license as shown in Figure 5-7.

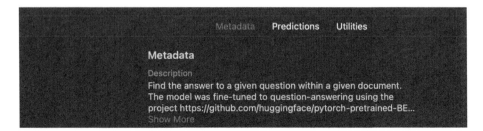

Figure 5-7. *BERTQA Model Metadata 2 in Xcode*

The Predictions section shows the inputs and outputs of the model as seen in Figure 5-8.

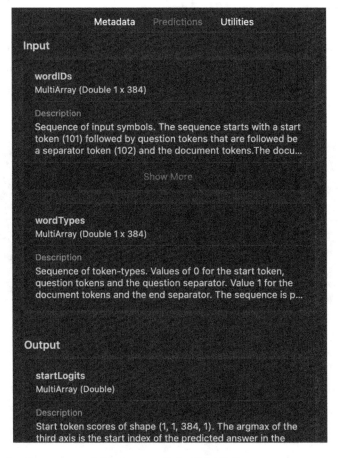

Figure 5-8. *Inputs and Outputs of the Model*

Here, we see our model takes two MultiArray, namely, wordIDs and wordTypes. Both arrays have a length of 384.

WordIDs are token indices, numerical representations of tokens building the sequences that will be used as input by the model. Figure 5-9 shows these sample indices of the words.

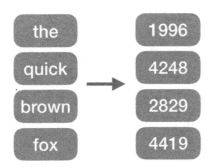

Figure 5-9. *Tokenizing the Words*

WordTypes, the other input of the model, are the token types. WordTypes tell the BERT model which elements of wordIDs are from the document.

The first and second inputs of the model are both padded with 0 values to length 384 to ensure they have a length of 384.

The outputs of the model are two MultiArray: startLogits and endLogits. They have a shape of (1, 1, 384, 1). The third axis has 384 numbers, and the maximum value in this third axis shows the index. For startLogits, it shows the predicted start index of the answer in the input sequence, and endLogits shows the predicted end index of the answer.

So if we oversimplify, the model takes 384 tokens that include a question and the paragraph and returns the start and end indices of the answer in a paragraph.

Another way to examine Core ML models is to use the Netron app. It is a viewer for neural network models. You can download it from here: `www.electronjs.org/apps/netron`.

It presents a more detailed view by showing every layer of the neural network. If you open the BERT-SQuAD model in Netron, you see the model as shown in Figure 5-10.

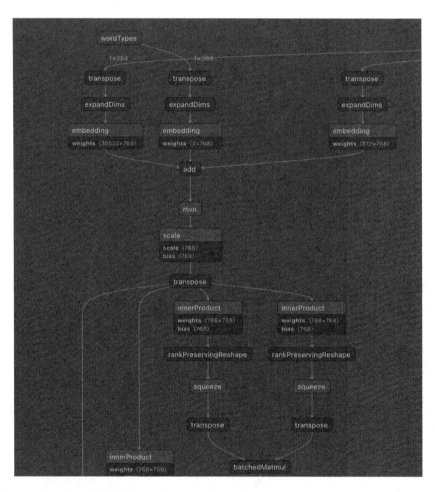

Figure 5-10. *BERT-SQuAD model in Netron*

With this app, you can have a deeper look into the architecture of the model and check the layer types and parameters.

Let's Build the App

We will build a single-view SwiftUI application that has a text view to paste the paragraph and a text field to write a question. When the user taps the "Find" button, we will use the BERT-SQuAD model to find the answer to the question in the given paragraph.

The final app will look like as shown in Figure 5-11.

Figure 5-11. *Final Look of Question-Answering App*

Download the start project from here: `https://github.com/ozgurshn/Chapter5-QuestionAnswering/tree/master/Starter`. Open the project in Xcode to start coding. In this project, many tedious tasks are done on your behalf so you can focus on the main parts. You can find the completed version of the project here: `https://github.com/ozgurshn/Chapter5-QuestionAnswering/tree/master/Final`.

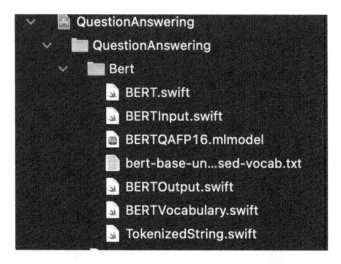

Figure 5-12. *BERT Files in the Project*

Using the BERT Model in iOS

You will see the "Bert" folder in this starter project as shown in Figure 5-12. Its files are the necessary files to run this model in iOS. These files are taken from Apple's sample project (`https://developer.apple.com/documentation/coreml/finding_answers_to_questions_in_a_text_document`). We will use these classes in our project, and I will explain all of these files one by one. Drag and drop the BERTQA model you downloaded before into the Bert folder.

The BERTQAFP16.mlmodel file is the BERT model in Core ML format that we inspected earlier.

The BERTInput class transforms the input data into model input format. Open the BERTInput.swift file and have a look at its init function.

It takes two string parameters: documentString and questionString as shown in Listing 5-1.

Listing 5-1. Init Function of BERTInput Class

```
init(documentString: String, questionString:
String) {

        document = TokenizedString(documentString)

        question = TokenizedString(questionString)
```

Its main function is to convert these two string parameters into model input format (wordIDs and wordTypes). Firstly, it separates text into words using NLTagger. It breaks up a string into word tokens, each of which is a substring of the original as shown in Listing 5-2.

Listing 5-2. Tokenization

```
        private static func wordTokens(from
rawString: String) -> [Substring] {

        // Store the tokenized substrings into an array.

        var wordTokens = [Substring]()

        // Use Natural Language's NLTagger to
tokenize the input by word.

        let tagger = NLTagger(tagSchemes:
[.tokenType])

        tagger.string = rawString
```

```
      // Find all tokens in the string and append
to the array.

      tagger.enumerateTags(in:
rawString.startIndex..<rawString.endIndex,

                              unit: .word,

                              scheme: .tokenType,

                              options:
[.omitWhitespace]) { (_, range) -> Bool in

          wordTokens.append(rawString[range])

          return true

      }

      return wordTokens

  }
```

Then, it finds the corresponding tokenId for each token using the tokenize function from the TokenizedString class. TokenIds are searched in a dictionary that built using the list in "bert-base-uncased- vocab.txt" file (Figure 5-13). This file has an index number for each word and separators.

ingAnswers	13239	##roy
EADME.md	13240	commissions
indingAnswers	13241	browns
Model	13242	##ania
BERT.swift	13243	destroyers
BERTInput.swift	13244	sheridan
BERTOutput.swift	13245	meadow
BERTVocabulary.swift	13246	##rius
TokenizedString.swift	13247	minerals
BERTQAFP16.mlmodel	13248	##cial
bert-base-un...sed-vocab.txt	13249	downstream
	13250	clash
	13251	gram

Figure 5-13. *Word List of Bert-Base*

Creating the wordID array is done by arranging the token IDs in the following order:

1. Starting token ID, which has a value of 101 and appears as "[CLS]" in the bert-base word list file

2. The token IDs from the question text

3. A separator token ID, which has a value of 102 and appears as "[SEP]" in the word list file

4. The token IDs from the text string

5. Another separator token ID ("[SEP]")

6. Padding token IDs to complete the 384 tokens if the resulting tokenID array's length is less than 384

The code of this instruction is shown in Listing 5-3.

Listing 5-3. Creating the WordID Array

```
// Start the wordID array with the `classification
start` token.

var wordIDs = [BERTVocabulary.classifyStartTokenID]

// Add the question tokens and a separator.

wordIDs += question.tokenIDs

wordIDs += [BERTVocabulary.separatorTokenID]

// Add the document tokens and a separator.

wordIDs += document.tokenIDs

wordIDs += [BERTVocabulary.separatorTokenID]

// Fill the remaining token slots with padding
tokens.

let tokenIDPadding = BERTInput.maxTokens -
wordIDs.count

wordIDs += Array(repeating:
BERTVocabulary.paddingTokenID, count: tokenIDPadding)

guard wordIDs.count == BERTInput.maxTokens else {

        fatalError("`wordIDs` array size isn't
the right size.")

    }
```

We converted the inputs (paragraph, question) into requested format for the model. Now, we need to feed the model with these inputs and perform prediction with this data. Open the BERT.swift file to check the implementation. It creates an instance of the BERT-SQuAD model using the code in Listing 5-4.

Listing 5-4. Creating the Model Instance

```
    let bertModel = try?
BERTQAFP16(configuration: MLModelConfiguration())
```

Check the "findAnswer" function. It's the function that takes the paragraph and question as inputs and returns the answer. It converts these parameters (paragraph, question) to BERTInput format that we analyzed earlier. After creating the requested input, we perform the prediction on the BERT model using the code in Listing 5-5.

Listing 5-5. Prediction on the BERT Model

```
    guard let prediction = try?
bertModel?.prediction(input: modelInput) else {

    return "The BERT model is unable to make a
prediction."
}

// Analyze the output form the BERT model.

guard let bestLogitIndices = bestLogitsIndices(from:
prediction,

                                        in:

bertInput.documentRange) else {

    return "Couldn't find a valid answer. Please try
again."

}
// Find the indices of the original string.

let documentTokens = bertInput.document.tokens
```

```
let answerStart =
documentTokens[bestLogitIndices.start].startIndex
```

```
let answerEnd =
documentTokens[bestLogitIndices.end].endIndex
```

```
// Return the portion of the original string as the
answer.
```

```
let originalText = bertInput.document.original
```

```
return originalText[answerStart..<answerEnd]
```

The model returns the confidence scores for the start and end index predictions in the given 384 tokens. It returns startLogits and endLogits for start and end index predictions. We need to find the highest values in each list. The "bestLogitsIndices" function finds the highest-valued pair of start and end indices, and this shows the location of the answer. The illustration of this process is shown in Figure 5-14.

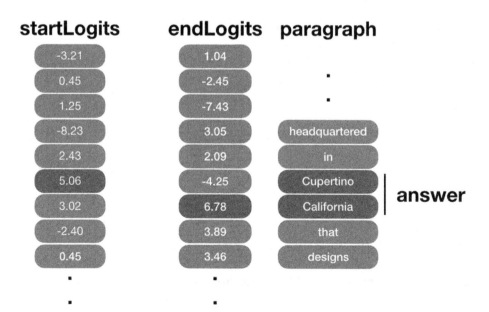

Figure 5-14. *Finding the Location of the Answer*

We find the highest confidence score in the startLogits list that shows the start location of the answer and the highest in the endLogits list that shows the end of the answer. We slice this part in the paragraph and return as an answer.

Building the UI of the App

We learned how to use the BERT-SQuAD model in iOS. Now, we will create the user interface of the app and use the question-answering model.

Open the ContentView.swift file. This is the main view of our SwiftUI app. We will add three UI elements: a text view for the paragraph, a text field for the question, and a button to start searching for the answer. We will highlight the answer in the paragraph with a yellow background if any answer exists.

For iOS 14, SwiftUI has built-in TextEditor, but that does not support attributed text. We want to highlight the answer in text using attributed text, so we will use UIKit's TextView by creating a SwiftUI wrapper for it. Open the TextView.swift file and copy the code in Listing 5-6.

Listing 5-6. Creating TextView

```
import SwiftUI

struct TextView: UIViewRepresentable {

    @Binding var
attributedText:NSMutableAttributedString

    func makeUIView(context: Context) -> UITextView {

        let textView = UITextView()

        return textView

    }
```

```
func updateUIView(_ uiView: UITextView, context:

                    Context) {

    uiView.attributedText = attributedText

}

}
```

UIViewRepresentable lets us wrap UIKit views and use them in SwiftUI. Two functions need to be filled: makeUIView which creates the view and updateUIView which shows SwiftUI which elements should be updated. Here, we bind the attributedText variable to TextView's attributedText property so it automatically shows the changes in UI.

Open the ContentView.swift file. Start with declaring the state variables in the ContentView class that will be bound to UI elements. We will create an attributed text for the paragraph; we can change the font in some parts of the attributed string. This will allow us to highlight the answer.

We create a variable for the question with a default value, but also the user can type any question. Finally, we create the BERT model instance to use our question-answering model as shown in Listing 5-7.

Listing 5-7. Create the State Variables

```
@State var attributedText =
NSMutableAttributedString(string: "Apple Inc. is an
American multinational technology company
headquartered in Cupertino, California, that designs,
develops, and sells consumer electronics, computer
software, and online services. It is considered one
of the Big Tech technology companies, alongside
Amazon, Google, Microsoft and Facebook. The company's
hardware products include the iPhone smartphone, the
iPad tablet computer, the Mac personal computer, the
```

iPod portable media player, the Apple Watch
smartwatch, the Apple TV digital media player, the
AirPods wireless earbuds and the HomePod smart
speaker. Apple's software includes macOS, iOS,
iPadOS, watchOS, and tvOS operating systems, the
iTunes media player, the Safari web browser, the
Shazam music identifier, and the iLife and iWork
creativity and productivity suites, as well as
professional applications like Final Cut Pro, Logic
Pro, and Xcode. Its online services include the
iTunes Store, the iOS App Store, Mac App Store, Apple
Music, Apple TV+, iMessage, and iCloud. Other
services include Apple Store, Genius Bar, AppleCare,
Apple Pay, Apple Pay Cash, and Apple Card.")

```
    @State var question = "Where is Apple Inc?"

    let bert = BERT()
```

In the body part of the ContentView class, we will put the UI elements
that we want to show on the screen. We start creating VStack to put
elements in order vertically. Then, we add the TextView we created
before and bind it to the attributedText state variable. When we update
attributedText, TextView will automatically update the UI and show the
text. Users will use this text view to paste the article that they want to
search in. We used the text view instead of a text field because it supports
multiline text and is better for long texts like articles. The other element we
add is a text field where the user will write their question, and we bind its
text to the question variable as shown in Listing 5-8.

Listing 5-8. Adding UI Elements

```
var body: some View {

    VStack

        {

            TextView(attributedText:
$attributedText)

            TextField("Enter your question",text:
$question)

        }

}
```

Now, we have two UI elements: a text view for the article and a text field for the question.

Under the text field, we will add a button to start searching. Copy the button code in Listing 5-9 under the text field.

Listing 5-9. Adding the Search Button

```
    Button(action: {

    // Run the search in the background to keep the
UI responsive.

    DispatchQueue.global(qos: .userInitiated).async {

    // Use the BERT model to search for the
answer.

    let answer = self.bert.findAnswer(for:
self.question, in: self.attributedText.string)
```

```
    // Update the UI on the main queue.

    DispatchQueue.main.async {

        let mutableAttributedText =
NSMutableAttributedString(string:
self.attributedText.string)

        let location =
answer.startIndex.utf16Offset(in:
self.attributedText.string)

        let length =
answer.endIndex.utf16Offset(in:
self.attributedText.string) - location

        let answerRange = NSRange(location:
location, length: length)

        let fullTextColor = UIColor.red

mutableAttributedText.addAttributes([.foregroundColor
: fullTextColor, .backgroundColor:UIColor.yellow],

range: answerRange)

            self.attributedText =
mutableAttributedText

        }

        print(String(answer))

        self.speechToText(text: String(answer))

        }
}){Text("Find")}.padding()
```

We created a button with a label "Find". When the user taps the button, its action is called. In this action, we call the "findAnswer" function of the BERT class with the parameters of the paragraph and a question. This call is made in a separate queue (userInitiated) so as not to block the main UI thread. After the model returns the results, we update the UI in the main thread by calling DispatchQueue.main.async. This ensures UI updates are handled properly. In this main thread call, we create a new attributed string from the paragraph text and find the start and end indices of the answer in this paragraph text. We create a range (NSRange) with start and end indices and use this index to color the background of the answer in the paragraph. We color the answer red and its background yellow.

You can now run the project on a simulator or on a device to test your application. As we fill the paragraph and the question with some text, it will show them. Tap the "Find" button to find the answer in the paragraph. As shown in Figure 5-15, it will highlight "Cupertino, California" in the paragraph as a response to the "Where is Apple Inc.?" question.

Figure 5-15. *Question-Answering App*

Congratulations! You just built a smart app that can find an answer in a text in seconds, and you have learned how to use a state-of-the-art natural language model in your iOS applications.

Next, we will add speech-to-text ability which allows us to ask a question using our voice and then use text-to-speech to make Siri read the answer.

Speech Recognition with the Speech Framework

You need to add two keys (NSSpeechRecognitionUsageDescription, NSMicrophoneUsageDescription) and their descriptions to the Info.plist file. These descriptions will be shown to the user when iOS asks the user to use a microphone and speech recognition. We will ask for transcription permission when the view appears. Add this function to request permission in your ContentView class.

Listing 5-10. Transcription Permission

```
func requestTranscribePermissions() {

    SFSpeechRecognizer.requestAuthorization
{ authStatus in

            DispatchQueue.main.async {

                if authStatus == .authorized {

                    print("Authorized for
transcription")

                } else {

                    print("Transcription permission
was declined.")

                }

            }

        }

    }
```

We will call this function when the main VStack appears. At the end of the VStack call, this function is as shown in Listing 5-11.

Listing 5-11. Permission Request

```
.onAppear{

        self.requestTranscribePermissions()

    }
```

We will use the SFSpeech framework to transcribe audio to text. Add the following declarations to the head of the ContentView struct:

```
private var recognitionTask: SFSpeechRecognitionTask?

private let audioEngine = AVAudioEngine()

private let speechRecognizer =
SFSpeechRecognizer(locale: Locale(identifier: "en- US"))!
```

In the preceding code, we created the recognitionTask variable, and we declared it here to store it between different sessions of speaking. This way, we can cancel previous tasks when we start a new speaking session. We also declared AVAudioEngine to process microphone audio stream and created a SFSpeechRecognizer for English to perform speech recognition.

Now, we will create the actual transcription function. Add the code in Listing 5-12 to the ContentView struct.

Listing 5-12. Audio Transcription with the Speech Framework

```
func transcribe(completionHandler: @escaping
(String)->()) {

        // Cancel the previous task if it's running.

        recognitionTask?.cancel()
```

```
    recognitionTask = nil

    // Configure the audio session for the app.

    let audioSession =
AVAudioSession.sharedInstance()

        try? audioSession.setCategory(.record,
mode: .measurement, options: .duckOthers)

        try? audioSession.setActive(true,
options: .notifyOthersOnDeactivation)

    let inputNode = audioEngine.inputNode

    // Create and configure the speech
recognition request.

    let recognitionRequest =
SFSpeechAudioBufferRecognitionRequest()

    recognitionRequest.shouldReportPartialResults
= true

    // Create a recognition task for the speech
recognition session.

    // Keep a reference to the task so that it
can be canceled.

    recognitionTask =
speechRecognizer.recognitionTask(with:
recognitionRequest) { result, error in
        if let result = result {
```

```
            print("Text \
(result.bestTranscription.formattedString)")

completionHandler(result.bestTranscription.formattedS tring)

        }

    }

    // Configure the microphone input.

    let recordingFormat =
inputNode.outputFormat(forBus: 0)

        inputNode.installTap(onBus: 0, bufferSize:
1024, format: recordingFormat) { (buffer:
AVAudioPCMBuffer, when: AVAudioTime) in

            recognitionRequest.append(buffer)

        }

    audioEngine.prepare()

    try? audioEngine.start()

    print("Ready to transcribe")

}
```

In the preceding code, we cancel previous recognition tasks and start
a new one. We create an audio session to process microphone input and
create a SFSpeechAudioBufferRecognitionRequest instance to transcribe
the audio. We set the shouldReportPartialResults parameter of this request
to true to receive partial results of each utterance. This lets us update the
text field with the partial result and keep the user informed. We return
the entire transcription of all utterances with result.bestTranscription.
formattedString.

To shorten the code, many exceptions are ignored in this code sample. In production apps, we should catch and handle exceptions properly with a do-try-catch block.

To call this transcribe function, we will add another button with a label "Speak." When the user taps this button, we will process the voice and change the question string. Add the button code in Listing 5-13 under the previous button and wrap these buttons in HStack to show them side by side.

Listing 5-13. Speak Button

```
Button(action:{

    self.transcribe { (speechText) in

        self.question = speechText

    }

}){Text("Speak")}
```

This button calls the transcribe function when tapped, and when the method returns a completion handler, it updates the question with this text. Now, run the project and test on a device. It should first ask for permission to use the microphone and to transcribe. Tap the "Speak" button and ask your question. What you say should appear in the question field. The result should look like what is shown in Figure 5-16.

Figure 5-16. *Speech Processing App*

The last thing we will add is text-to-speech capability. This will speak the found answer in the paragraph. Add the code in Listing 5-14 in the ContentView struct.

Listing 5-14. Text-to-Speech

```
func speechToText(text:String)

    {

        let utterance = AVSpeechUtterance(string:
text)
```

```
    utterance.voice =
AVSpeechSynthesisVoice(language: "en-GB")

    let synthesizer = AVSpeechSynthesizer()

    synthesizer.speak(utterance)

}
```

In the preceding code, we create an AVSpeechUtterance instance with the text. Using this class, we can change the accent of the voice or speaking rate. Lastly, we create AVSpeechSynthesizer to speak the answer. That's all to add text-to-speech capability to your app.

We will call this function as shown in Listing 5-15 where we handle the result of the "findAnswer" method under the "Find" button's action.

Listing 5-15. Calling the Text-to-Speech Function

```
print(String(answer))
```

```
self.speechToText(text: String(answer))
```

Our app is ready to speak. Test it on a device, tap the "Speak" button, and ask your question and then tap the "Find" button. It will find and highlight the answer in the article and also speak the answer.

Summary

In this chapter, we worked on the BERT model; we learned how it works, what are its inputs and outputs, and how it tokenizes the strings. The BERT-SQuAD model and the dataset (SQuAD 2.0) that this model used are also covered in this chapter. We also learned how to examine the Core

ML models using Xcode or the Netron application. We built the question-answering app using SwiftUI and the BERT-SQuAD model and learned how to integrate NLP models into our iOS applications. Moreover, speech recognition and text-to-speech capabilities have been added using the Speech framework to make our app smarter.

CHAPTER 6

Text Summarization

This chapter will cover text summarization using natural language processing techniques. Different types of text summarization techniques will be introduced with examples. You will gain the intuition behind summarization and be able to apply it to your iOS projects. After gaining the principal knowledge, we will use the built-in NLP capabilities in iOS to develop a smart iOS application that can summarize the given article.

What Is Text Summarization?

Text summarization is the process of shortening text computationally, to create a subset that represents the most significant information within the original content. Text summarization tries to find the most informative sentences in an article and extract this information. Text summarization is usually categorized into two techniques: extractive summarization and abstractive summarization.

Extractive summarization is performed by finding the most important sentences from the text and extracting those sentences as shown in Figure 6-1. In this technique, sentences are scored based on their importance, and the top k most important sentences are stitched together to create a summary. Original sentences are used in the summary without any paraphrasing.

© Özgür Sahin 2021
Ö. Sahin, *Develop Intelligent iOS Apps with Swift*,
https://doi.org/10.1007/978-1-4842-6421-8_6

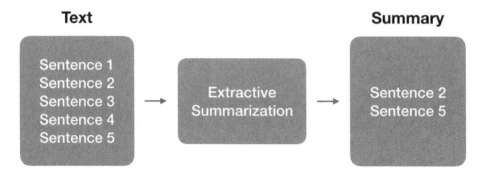

Figure 6-1. *Extractive Summarization*

Abstractive text summarization interprets the text using natural language techniques and generates a new shorter text as shown in Figure 6-2. This is a more complicated method as it requires a general understanding of the content and paraphrasing the critical information in a shorter text. The summary generated using this technique is closer to what humans may express as a summary. Recently, abstractive methods started to take advantage of the developments in deep learning.

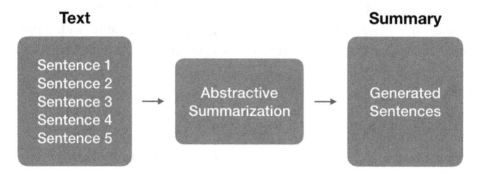

Figure 6-2. *Abstractive Summarization*

The app that we will develop in this chapter uses an extractive summarization technique. We will find the high-scored sentences and represent the text with these sentences.

We will not develop an abstractive summarization sample in this chapter, but you can develop it using the sequence-to-sequence (Seq2Seq) model by training on the summarization dataset with one of the deep learning frameworks (Keras, PyTorch, etc.) and convert it to Core ML format using coremltools.

Let's get our hands dirty and build the text summarizer app using the extractive summarization method. I recommend you to complete it yourself, but if you feel lazy, you can find the completed project of this chapter here: `https://github.com/ozgurshn/Chapter6-TextSummarizer`.

Building the Text Summarizer App

Start with creating an empty SwiftUI project in Xcode. Choose "App" template and make sure the user interface is set to SwiftUI as shown in Figure 6-3.

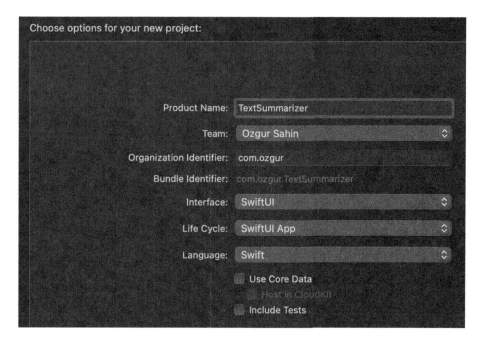

Figure 6-3. *New Project*

Firstly, we will create a text view to show the article that we want to summarize. SwiftUI provides TextEditor instead of TextView of UIKit. Create a Swift file named "TextView.swift" and copy the code in Listing 6-1.

ContentView is our main view. Let's open it and design the screen. Copy the code in Listing 6-1 into the ContentView file.

Listing 6-1. ContentView

```
struct ContentView: View {

    @State var text = ""

    @State var summary = ""

    var body: some View {

        VStack

        {

            TextEditor(text:$text)

            Button(action:{

                self.summary =
Summarizer().summarize(text:self.text)

            }){

                Text("Summarize")

            }

            TextEditor(text:$summary)

        }

    }

}
```

In the ContentView, we created two state properties to hold text and summary. They are created as a state because we want them bound to UI and reflect the changes. In the body, the main element we use is the VStack that organizes UI elements vertically. Inside it, we placed a text editor for the article, a button to create a summary, and a text editor to show the summary. We left the button action empty, and we will fill it after writing the text summarizer class.

Let's check the app to see if everything is working. Unless preview is visible, open Canvas to see the preview as shown in Figure 6-4. Click Editor ➤ Canvas from the menu or use the option+command+enter shortcut.

Figure 6-4. *SwiftUI Preview Testing*

Create a Swift file called "Summarizer.swift". In this class, we will handle the text summarization process by scoring the sentences in an article and creating a summary based on high-scored sentences.

Import the Natural Language framework as shown in Listing 6-2, we will use it to tokenize the article.

Listing 6-2. Import the Natural Language Framework

```
import NaturalLanguage
```

Then we create a struct to hold sentences and their rank and index as shown in Listing 6-3. Rank shows the importance of the sentence, and index shows the place of the sentence in the article.

Listing 6-3. SentenceAndRank

```
struct SentenceAndRank

{

    var sentence:String

    var rank:Int

    var index:Int
}
```

Then let's create a class called Summarizer and declare our stop words as shown in Listing 6-4.

Listing 6-4. Stop Words

```
class Summarizer

{

    let stopWords = ["a", "about", "above", "across",
"after", "afterwards", "again", "against", "all",
"almost", "alone", "along", "already", "also",
"although", "always", "am", "among", "amongst",
"amoungst", "amount", "an", "and", "another", "any",
"anyhow", "anyone", "anything", "anyway",
"anywhere", "are", "around", "as", "at", "back",
"be", "became", "because", "become", "becomes",
```

"becoming", "been", "before", "beforehand", "behind",
"being", "below", "beside", "besides", "between",
"beyond", "bill", "both", "bottom", "but", "by",
"call", "can", "cannot", "cant", "co", "con",
"could", "couldnt", "cry", "de", "describe",
"detail", "do", "done", "down", "due", "during",
"each", "eg", "eight", "either", "eleven", "else",
"elsewhere", "empty", "enough", "etc", "even",
"ever", "every", "everyone", "everything",
"everywhere", "except", "few", "fifteen", "fify",
"fill", "find", "fire", "first", "five", "for",
"former", "formerly", "forty", "found", "four",
"from", "front", "full", "further", "get", "give",
"go", "had", "has", "hasnt", "have", "he", "hence",
"her", "here", "hereafter", "hereby", "herein",
"hereupon", "hers", "herself", "him", "himself",
"his", "how", "however", "hundred", "ie", "if", "in",
"inc", "indeed", "interest", "into", "is", "it",
"its", "itself", "keep", "last", "latter",
"latterly", "least", "less", "ltd", "made", "many",
"may", "me", "meanwhile", "might", "mill", "mine",
"more", "moreover", "most", "mostly", "move", "much",
"must", "my", "myself", "name", "namely", "neither",
"never", "nevertheless", "next", "nine", "no",
"nobody", "none", "noone", "nor", "not", "nothing",
"now", "nowhere", "of", "off", "often", "on", "once",
"one", "only", "onto", "or", "other", "others",
"otherwise", "our", "ours", "ourselves", "out",
"over", "own", "part", "per", "perhaps", "please",
"put", "rather", "re", "same", "see", "seem",
"seemed", "seeming", "seems", "serious", "several",

```
"she", "should", "show", "side", "since", "sincere",
"six", "sixty", "so", "some", "somehow", "someone",
"something", "sometime", "sometimes", "somewhere",
"still", "such", "system", "take", "ten", "than",
"that", "the", "their", "them", "themselves", "then",
"thence", "there", "thereafter", "thereby",
"therefore", "therein", "thereupon", "these", "they",
"thickv", "thin", "third", "this", "those", "though",
"three", "through", "throughout", "thru", "thus",
"to", "together", "too", "top", "toward", "towards",
"twelve", "twenty", "two", "un", "under", "until",
"up", "upon", "us", "very", "via", "was", "we",
"well", "were", "what", "whatever", "when", "whence",
"whenever", "where", "whereafter", "whereas",
"whereby", "wherein", "whereupon", "wherever",
"whether", "which", "while", "whither", "who",
"whoever", "whole", "whom", "whose", "why", "will",
"with", "within", "without", "would", "yet", "you",
"your", "yours", "yourself", "yourselves"]
```

}

Stop words are the most common words in a language. Usually, we filter out these words before processing the text. As we will measure sentence importance based on word frequencies, these words may have a negative effect because they are the most frequent words.

Then, we create a text splitting function to split the given text into sentences or words. We use NLTokenizer from the Natural Language framework to enumerate tokens (words, sentences, etc.) as shown in Listing 6-5. Create a list of these tokens and return this list.

Listing 6-5. Text Splitting Function

```
    private func splitTo(text:String,
unit:NLTokenUnit) -> [String]

    {

        let tokenizer = NLTokenizer(unit: unit)

        tokenizer.string = text

        var tokens = [String]()

        tokenizer.enumerateTokens(in:
text.startIndex..<text.endIndex) { range, _ in

            tokens.append(String(text[range]))
            return true

        }

        return tokens

    }
```

Next, we will create a function that will calculate the frequencies (occurrence count) of the words in a given text as shown in Listing 6-6. We use NSLinguisticTagger to enumerate the words in the text. We ignore punctuation and whitespaces by specifying NSLinguisticTagger. Options. We use lowercase versions of the words to standardize the words on the list. Enumeration is performed using the enumerate function of NSLinguisticTagger. The word counts are placed in a dictionary and returned.

Listing 6-6. Calculating Word Frequencies

```swift
private func calculateWordFrequencies(text: String)
-> [String: Int] {

    var frequencyList = [String: Int]()

    let tagger = NSLinguisticTagger(tagSchemes:
[.tokenType], options: 0)

    let range = NSRange(location: 0, length:
text.utf16.count)

    let options: NSLinguisticTagger.Options =
[.omitPunctuation, .omitWhitespace]

    tagger.string = text.lowercased()

    tagger.enumerateTags(in: range, unit: .word,
scheme: .tokenType, options: options) { _,
tokenRange, _ in

        let word = (text as NSString).substring(with:
tokenRange)

        if frequencyList[word] != nil {

            frequencyList[word]! += 1

        } else {

            frequencyList[word] = 1

        }

    }

    return frequencyList

}
```

For example, if we calculate the word frequencies for the article about Apple from Wikipedia, we can see that the most frequent words are stop words like "and" and "the" as shown in Figure 6-5.

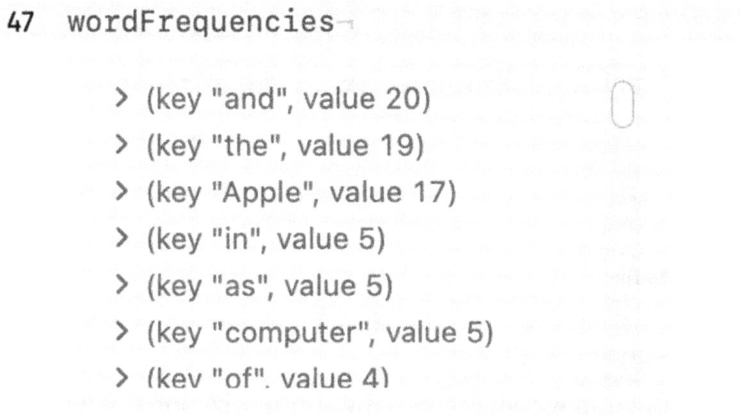

```
47  wordFrequencies

        > (key "and", value 20)
        > (key "the", value 19)
        > (key "Apple", value 17)
        > (key "in", value 5)
        > (key "as", value 5)
        > (key "computer", value 5)
        > (key "of", value 4)
```

Figure 6-5. *Word Frequencies*

Now, we need to calculate the sum of the words' frequencies for a given sentence. This will show sentence importance. Here, we assume that the most informative words are often repeated in an article, but we ignore the stop words as they are very frequent. Listing 6-7 showns how to create this function.

Listing 6-7. Calculate Word Frequency Sum of a Sentence

```
private func getWordFrequencySum(sentence:String,
frequencies:[String:Int])->Int

{

    let wordList = splitTo(text: sentence,
unit: .word)

    var rank = 0
```

```
    for word in wordList

    {

        if !stopWords.contains(word)

        {
            rank += frequencies[word, default: 0]

        }

    }

    return rank

}
```

The last function we will write is the summarization function. As shown in Listing 6-8, we calculate each word's frequency in the given text and then split the article into sentences. We loop through the sentences and calculate each sentence's word frequency sum. Then we sort the list in descending order according to sentences' ranks. We select the top three high-rank sentences and append them together according to their indices.

Listing 6-8. Summarization Function

```
func summarize(text:String)->String

{

    let wordFrequencies =
calculateWordFrequencies(text: text)

    let sentences = splitTo(text: text,
unit: .sentence)

    var sentenceAndRank:[SentenceAndRank] = []
```

```
for (index, sentence) in sentences.enumerated()

{

    let rank = getWordFrequencySum(sentence:
sentence,frequencies: wordFrequencies)

sentenceAndRank.append(SentenceAndRank(sentence:
sentence, rank: rank, index:index))

}

// Sort Sentences by ranking

let sentencesByRanking = sentenceAndRank.sorted {
$0.rank > $1.rank }

// Select the most important 3 sentences

let keySentences = sentencesByRanking.prefix(3)

//return in sentence order and merge all
sentences into one sentence

return keySentences.sorted {$0.index <
$1.index }.map{$0.sentence}.joined()

}
```

The summarization class is ready to summarize the text. The last thing we have to do is to call this function from ContentView. Open the ContentView and call the "summarize" function from the button's action as shown in Listing 6-9.

Listing 6-9. Summarize Button Action

```
Button(action:{

            self.summary =
Summarizer().summarize(text:self.text)

        })
```

Run your app on a simulator or SwiftUI live preview. Copy some long text to your first text editor and tap the "Summarize" button. The summary will be shown in the text editor under the button as shown in Figure 6-6.

Figure 6-6. *Text Summarizer App*

Summary

In this chapter, we covered the essential text summarization techniques using natural language processing. Abstractive and extractive summarization methods have been introduced. After gaining theoretical knowledge, we built a text summarizer app using the extractive summarization technique and built-in NLP capabilities in iOS. While developing the app, we learned how to filter out common words or stop words and how to use NSLinguisticTagger to calculate word frequencies.

CHAPTER 7

Integrating Keras Models

This chapter will cover advanced use cases where you will integrate models trained in third-party deep learning frameworks like Keras. You can train models using Create ML easily, but sometimes you may want to use new deep learning architecture that does not exist in Create ML. For these use cases, we will learn how to integrate Keras models into our application. In this chapter, we will convert the Keras model to Core ML format using the coremltools library. A sample text classification application will be developed to learn by doing. You will also learn to use the Google Colab service which is an online and free Python environment.

Converting the Keras Model into Core ML Format

Keras is a wrapper over more complicated deep learning libraries like TensorFlow or Theano. Its code writing style is simpler and more intuitive than the libraries it wraps. It lets easy and fast prototyping and supports multiple neural network architectures.

In this section, we will train the model on Google Colab. It is a free online platform to train your neural networks and run your experiments. It also offers free powerful GPU for faster training. You can also run these

© Özgür Sahin 2021
Ö. Sahin, *Develop Intelligent iOS Apps with Swift*,
https://doi.org/10.1007/978-1-4842-6421-8_7

samples in the local virtual environment that we created in earlier chapters if you want to train your PC, but I recommend using Colab. Colab also uses Jupyter notebooks, but they are hosted by Google. With these notebooks, we can execute our codes cell by cell and see the results immediately.

Go to https://colab.research.google.com/ and create a new notebook (File ➤ New notebook). Copy-paste and run the code in Listing 7-1 to install the libraries. Normally, TensorFlow and Keras are both installed in Colab, but we reinstall because their versions are noncompatible with the coremltools. You run into some problems if you use the currently installed versions in Colab.

Training the Text Classification Model in Keras

Copy the code in Listing 7-1 into a cell in Colab.

Listing 7-1. Install the Libraries

```
!pip install tensorflow==1.14

!pip install keras==2.2.4

!pip install coremltools==3.4
```

To run the cell, just click the play button on the left which is shown in Figure 7-1. During the execution, you will see a rotating cycle.

```
1 !pip install tensorflow==1.14
2 !pip install keras==2.2.4
3 !pip install coremltools==3.4
```

Figure 7-1. *Google Colab Cell*

After running the preceding cell, we will run the code in Listing 7-2 to import the libraries. Copy the code into a new code cell and run it.

Listing 7-2. Import the Libraries

```
import numpy as np

from keras.preprocessing.text import Tokenizer

from keras.preprocessing.sequence import
pad_sequences

from keras.models import Sequential, Model

from keras.layers import Dense, Input, Bidirectional,
GRU, TimeDistributed, Activation, Flatten, Embedding

from keras.optimizers import Adam

from keras.datasets import imdb
```

Here, we imported NumPy to use its array functions, and also we imported the text tokenizer and the specific layers of the Keras library. Lastly, we imported the IMDB dataset from Keras datasets. The Keras. datasets (`https://keras.io/api/datasets/`) module provides a few toy datasets (already vectorized, in NumPy format) so you don't need to deal with downloading, unzipping, and processing the data.

We will use the IMDB movie review sentiment classification dataset to train a classification model. According to the Keras documentation, this is a dataset of 25,000 movie reviews from IMDB, labeled by sentiment (positive/negative).

Reviews have been preprocessed, and each review is encoded as a list of word indices (integers) as shown in Figure 7-2. For convenience, words are indexed by overall frequency in the dataset, so that, for instance, the integer "3" encodes the third most frequent word in the data. This allows for quick filtering operations such as "only consider the top 10,000 most common words, but eliminate the top 20 most common words."

```
'seriously': 612,
'sugercoma': 52369,
'grimstead': 52370,
"'fairy'": 52371,
'zenda': 30611,
"'twins'": 52372,
'realisation': 17640,
'highsmith': 27664,
'raunchy': 7817,
'incentives': 40965,
'flatson': 52374,
'snooker': 35097,
'crazies': 16829,
'crazier': 14902,
'grandma': 7094,
'napunsaktha': 52375,
'workmanship': 30612,
'reisner': 52376,
"sanford's": 61306,
```

Figure 7-2. *Word Representations in the IMDB Dataset*

We will take the top 10000 most common words from this dataset and train a model using this data. The code in Listing 7-3 shows how to load this data from Keras datasets. Copy the code into a new cell and run it.

Listing 7-3. Load the IMDB Dataset

```
#take most 10000 common words in the imdb dataset

maxNumberOfWords = 10000

##work around to load imdb dataset as imdb.load_data
didn't work directly for this version. https://
stackoverflow.com/a/56243777/4156490
```

```
##the error is 'ValueError: Object arrays cannot be
loaded when allow_pickle=False'

# save np.load

np_load_old = np.load

# modify the default parameters of np.load

np.load = lambda *a,**k: np_load_old(*a,

allow_pickle=True)

# call load_data with allow_pickle implicitly set to
true
(x_train, y_train), (x_test, y_test) =
imdb.load_data(num_words=maxNumberOfWords)

# restore np.load for future normal usage

np.load = np_load_old
```

Normally, the imdb.load_data function is enough to load the dataset, but for this version of TensorFlow, we need to implement a workaround solution. After this solution, we load the data and separate it into train and test subsets. The separation ratio is 0.5 by default, so we separate the dataset by half for train and test. The test dataset will not be used in training; it will be used in testing to see how good our trained model performs on data it has not been before. The parameters starting with x show the IMDB review and y the sentiment of that review.

Now that we have loaded our data, we will check the distribution of the number of words. We will create a Pandas data frame with the number of words in each review and plot the diagram. Copy-paste the code in Listing 7-4 and run it to create the diagram as shown in Figure 7-3.

Listing 7-4. Create a Distribution Graph

```
import matplotlib.pyplot as plt

import pandas as pd

text_word_count = []

# populate the lists with word count

for i in x_train:

  text_word_count.append(len(i))

length_df = pd.DataFrame({'text':text_word_count})

length_df.hist(bins = 30)

plt.show()
```

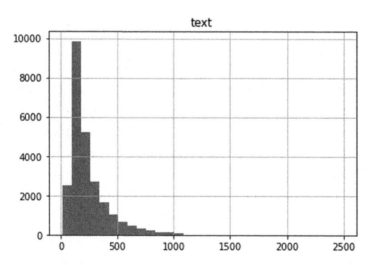

Figure 7-3. *Word Count Distribution*

Most of the reviews have fewer than 500 words as we see in the plot. We need to represent our words as small number of tokens as possible to make training time shorter. I choose 300 for this tutorial. We will represent reviews with 300 tokens and train a neural network model that takes 300 tokens as input.

Since our model takes a fixed-size input, we need to pad sequences to the fixed length. For the movie reviews that have fewer than 300 words, we will pad the rest with zeros as shown in Listing 7-5.

Listing 7-5. Pad Sequences with Zeros

```
maxlen = 300

x_train =
pad_sequences(x_train,maxlen=maxlen,padding='post')

x_test = pad_sequences(x_test,

maxlen = maxlen,padding='post')
```

In the preceding code, we state that we want to pad the sequences to the length 300, and we want zeros after the sequence. The default behavior of this method is to put zeros before the sequence, so we state it with a padding parameter.

We have prepared the input data. Now we can create the Keras model. For the model structure, I took the base code from Jacopo Mangiavacchi's implementation. Here, we will create a simple recurrent neural network (RNN)–based model for text classification.

RNN models suffer from the vanishing gradient problem during back-propagation. In each iteration, neural network weights are updated; and for the earlier layers, get a small gradient update and stop learning. Long short-term memory (LSTM) and GRU (Gated Recurrent Unit) aim to solve this problem.

We will use Gated Recurrent Unit (GRU). It is a type of RNN architecture that uses gates to control the flow of information between cells in the neural network. These gates are two vectors that decide which information should be passed to the output.

Listing 7-6. Creating the Keras Model

```
model = Sequential([

                    Embedding(maxNumberOfWords, 128,
input_length=maxlen),

                    GRU(128, batch_size=1,
return_sequences=True),

                    TimeDistributed(Dense(64)),

                    Activation('relu'),

                    TimeDistributed(Dense(32)),

                    Activation('relu'),

                    Flatten(),

                    Dense(1, activation='sigmoid')

                    ])

model.summary()
```

We use the Sequential class to stack layers of the model as shown in Listing 7-6. The embedding layer takes integer representations of the words from the IMDB dataset and turns them into fixed-size dense vectors. We set the input dimension of the embedding to the maximum number of words (vocabulary) and the dimension of the dense embedding to 128. Its input length is set to *maxlen* which is 300 for this training. It means the input sequence length will be 300.

After the embedding layer, we place the GRU layer with 128 units which sets the output size to 128. The return_sequences parameter returns the last output if set to true and returns the full sequence if set to false.

The TimeDistributed layer allows applying a layer to every temporal slice of an input. We use relu as an activation function and add 1 unit dense layer with sigmoid activation to the end of the layers. The output will be between 0 and 1. Lastly, we print the model's summary. We don't need to add print in Jupyter Notebook; it prints the output by default.

Printing the model's summary is useful to check your model's inputs, outputs, parameters, and data flow. Figure 7-4 shows the model's summary.

Layer (type)	Output Shape	Param #
embedding_4 (Embedding)	(None, 300, 128)	1280000
gru_4 (GRU)	(None, 300, 128)	98688
time_distributed_7 (TimeDist	(None, 300, 64)	8256
activation_8 (Activation)	(None, 300, 64)	0
time_distributed_8 (TimeDist	(None, 300, 32)	2080
activation_9 (Activation)	(None, 300, 32)	0
flatten_4 (Flatten)	(None, 9600)	0
dense_12 (Dense)	(None, 1)	9601

```
Total params: 1,398,625
Trainable params: 1,398,625
Non-trainable params: 0
```

Figure 7-4. *Model's Summary*

Our model is ready. We can compile and train the model. Compiling configures the model with losses and metrics and makes it ready for training. Copy-paste the code Listing 7-7 to compile and train your model.

Listing 7-7. Compile and Train the Model

```
model.compile(loss='binary_crossentropy',
optimizer='adam', metrics=['accuracy'])

model.fit(x_train, y_train, epochs=50,
validation_split=0.2)
```

In the compile method, we set the loss function to binary_crossentropy as we have only two classes (positive/negative). We use the Adam optimizer and accuracy as a metric. Metric is a function that is used to evaluate the performance of your model.

We use the fit method to train our model. Providing the validation data is optional here, but if you set it, you can track the validation metrics of your training.

Normally, we would use x_test and y_test for validation; but to make training shorter, I set validation_split to 0.2, to separate 20% of the training data for validation. The model is not trained with validation data; it is only used for evaluating the model at the end of each epoch. While the model is being trained, we can track the training results as seen in Figure 7-5.

```
Train on 20000 samples, validate on 5000 samples
Epoch 1/50
20000/20000 [==============================] - 230s 12ms/step - loss: 0.3766 - acc: 0.8173 - val_loss: 0.2793 - val_acc:
Epoch 2/50
20000/20000 [==============================] - 230s 12ms/step - loss: 0.1858 - acc: 0.9287 - val_loss: 0.2848 - val_acc:
Epoch 3/50
20000/20000 [==============================] - 230s 11ms/step - loss: 0.1108 - acc: 0.9580 - val_loss: 0.3112 - val_acc:
Epoch 4/50
```

Figure 7-5. *Training Results*

After training for 50 epochs, we reach 1.0 for the training accuracy (acc) and 0.8816 for the validation accuracy (val_acc). This means the model predicts %88 of the validation data (the data it hasn't seen before) correctly.

After training finishes, our model is ready to be used. We will convert it into Core ML format and export the model using the code in Listing 7-8.

Listing 7-8. Convert the Model to Core ML Format

```
import coremltools

coreml_model =
coremltools.converters.keras.convert(model,
input_names="input", output_names="output")

coreml_model.save('imdbGRU.mlmodel')
```

This code saves the mlmodel to the Colab environment. Click the folder icon on the left side to check and download the file.

Testing the Core ML Model

To ensure the conversion works smoothly, we need to make sure the converted model predicts the same values as the Keras model. We can't test the Core ML model in the Colab environment since it only runs on macOS. There are two ways to use your Core ML model for prediction. You can run it with Xcode, or you can run it using a Python environment and coremltools on macOS. I will show you both of them.

Firstly, we need a reference to test our model. To create this, I will use the Keras model to predict the sentiment of an arbitrary text. I will compare this value with the Core ML prediction and expect them to be the same. If they aren't producing the same result, that means the model is not converted properly.

Let's try it with some arbitrary text data. Firstly, we need to get words' integer representations in the IMDB dataset. The code in Listing 7-9 downloads this data in JSON format and loads it into a dictionary.

Listing 7-9. Loading Integer Representations of the Words

```
wordDictionary = imdb.get_word_index(

    path='imdb_word_index.json'
)
```

The dictionary that contains words and integer representations is shown in Figure 7-6.

```
'memoriam': 52198,
'inventively': 30592,
"levant's": 25249,
'portobello': 20638,
'remand': 52200,
'mummified': 19504,
'honk': 27650,
'spews': 19505,
```

Figure 7-6. *Word Embeddings*

The code in Listing 7-10 predicts the sentiment of this arbitrary text: "super cool." We find the integer representations from the dictionary and then pad them with zeros up to length 300 since we trained our model in this way.

Listing 7-10. Keras Model Prediction

```
paddedText = pad_sequences(

np.array([[wordDictionary["super"],wordDictionary["co
ol"]]]), maxlen=300,padding='post'

    )

model.predict(paddedText)
```

Running the preceding code produces the result [[0.6204907]]. Let's check if the converted model in Core ML format also creates this output for the same text input.

Testing the Core ML Model in Jupyter Notebook

Activate the virtual environment that you created in earlier chapters and create a Jupyter notebook. The code in Listing 7-11 uses the path of my virtual environment; don't forget to set it to your path.

Listing 7-11. Activate the Virtual Environment and Run Jupyter Notebook

```
cd environment/coremlenv/

source bin/activate

ipython notebook
```

This opens Jupyter Dashboards. Create a new Python 3 notebook there. Copy-paste the code in Listing 7-12 to load the Core ML model you converted before.

Listing 7-12. Load the Core ML Model

```
import coremltools as ct

# Load the model

model = ct.models.MLModel('/Users/ozgur/Downloads/
imdbGRU.mlmodel')
```

If you want to check your model specification, you can run the code in Listing 7-13. This prints the input and output types of your model.

Listing 7-13. Print Model Specs

```
# Get spec from the model

spec = model.get_spec()

# print input/output description for the model

print(spec.description)
```

Input and output description of the model looks like that in Figure 7-7. The model takes two inputs: input and gru_2_h_in with shapes 1 and 128. Its outputs are output and gr_2_h_out with shapes 1 and 128.

```
input {
  name: "input"
  type {
    multiArrayType {
      shape: 1
      dataType: DOUBLE
    }
  }
}
input {
  name: "gru_2_h_in"
  type {
    multiArrayType {
      shape: 128
      dataType: DOUBLE
    }
    isOptional: true
  }
}
output {
  name: "output"
  type {
    multiArrayType {
      shape: 1
      dataType: DOUBLE
    }
  }
}
output {
  name: "gru_2_h_out"
  type {
    multiArrayType {
      shape: 128
      dataType: DOUBLE
    }
  }
}
metadata {
  userDefined {
    key: "coremltoolsVersion"
    value: "3.4"
  }
}
```

Figure 7-7. *Model Specification*

By examining this spec, we figure out what to expect from our model, what to feed, and what it will produce. Now we can make the prediction using our Core ML model.

Listing 7-14. Prediction on the Core ML Model

```
from keras.preprocessing.sequence import
pad_sequences

from keras.preprocessing.sequence import
pad_sequences

import numpy as np

wordArray = np.array([[1162,643]])

paddedArray =
pad_sequences(wordArray,maxlen=300,padding='post')

reshapedArray = paddedArray.reshape(300,1,1)

print(model.predict({'input':reshapedArray}))
```

As shown in Listing 7-14, we use integer representations of the words "super" (1162) and "cool" (643) from the IMDB dataset. Using the pad_sequences function, we add zeros until the list count is 300. Then we reshape the array to (300,1,1) dimensions. If we don't reshape this array and use an array with shape (300), it produces the error shown in Listing 7-15 that states input size is not as expected.

Listing 7-15. Input Size Error

```
{

    NSLocalizedDescription = "For input feature
'input', the provided shape (1 \U00d7 300) is not
compatible with the model's feature description.";
```

```
    NSUnderlyingError = "Error
Domain=com.apple.CoreML Code=1 \"Neural Network
(<=version 3) inputs can only be of size 1, 3, or
5.\" UserInfo={NSLocalizedDescription=Neural Network (<=version
3) inputs can only be of size 1, 3, or
5.}";

}
```

We make a prediction with the reshaped array and print the output as shown in Figure 7-8.

```
{'gru_2_h_out': array([ 0.20340762, -0.32752663, -0.50733715, -0.11236852,  0.56811202,
        0.1797075 , -0.35158285, -0.19052231, -0.94519579, -0.00434176,
        0.03767665, -0.80087578,  0.19913661,  0.30841312, -0.29123729,
       -0.56617773, -0.80684507,  0.15600927,  0.12033027,  0.49665588,
       -0.38669786,  0.08598833, -0.25962713, -0.01011314, -0.07390687,
       -0.48079312, -0.70322716, -0.59781581, -0.13696411,  0.55333066,
       -0.19940589, -0.18909742,  0.04067411, -0.04610157, -0.23380621,
        0.30891472,  0.09603257, -0.60961127, -0.76701027, -0.02726669,
        0.34737778, -0.01563397,  0.52953273, -0.8644222 , -0.28230479,
        0.76521921,  0.1962359 ,  0.07846273, -0.35460466, -0.03217462,
       -0.1334807 , -0.27746779, -0.19590113,  0.3196888 , -0.00960168,
       -0.11077721, -0.04427606, -0.06867522,  0.37383848, -0.12203464,
       -0.47736654,  0.38310796, -0.44074407,  0.14550571, -0.25520846,
        0.70372784,  0.35896403,  0.07417729,  0.36929464, -0.26314798,
        0.18437898,  0.01186351, -0.05691416,  0.16893803,  0.00929269,
       -0.13004856, -0.1281752 ,  0.01959103,  0.54532963,  0.03286906,
       -0.8167147 , -0.03253212,  0.55529237, -0.43771237,  0.00322904,
        0.58515954,  0.16381149, -0.28827339,  0.08773626, -0.29513186,
       -0.00562361,  0.54068309,  0.18844116,  0.44450524,  0.24949285,
        0.44630995, -0.02912364, -0.25798005, -0.46619061, -0.17899188,
        0.14166987, -0.02741264,  0.00752871,  0.80752987, -0.29241979,
       -0.50226957,  0.1057559 , -0.0071598 , -0.18053509, -0.5881027 ,
        0.00676884,  0.184883  , -0.25979683,  0.29172781,  0.03165273,
       -0.57036126, -0.68262613, -0.48212206, -0.26851285,  0.22277518,
        0.20434873,  0.02046606, -0.20425695,  0.0577577 ,  0.19374152,
       -0.08971952, -0.15631853,  0.07466556]), 'output': array([0.62049049])}
```

Figure 7-8. *Model's Output*

Notice the last element named output and its value. It's the same result predicted when we made a prediction with the Keras model. So we made sure that our conversion is successful and the converted model works properly.

You can find the full code of this Colab notebook here: `https://colab.research.google.com/drive/1p4ArC9yN- mXp1D4YXWZHuKbfXKnJvk7O?usp=sharing`.

Testing the Core ML Model in Xcode

Create a new SwiftUI project with App template. Drag and drop the Core ML model into your project as shown in Figure 7-9. Usually, this kind of testing is performed with unit testing bundle, but the mlmodel's class is not usable in test projects in Xcode 12 even if it used to work in Xcode 11. Therefore, I will test it by debugging in Xcode 12.

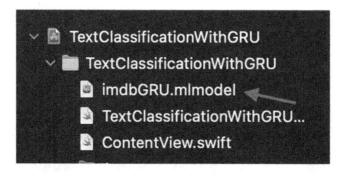

Figure 7-9. *Drag and Drop the Model*

Create a class called GRUModel and copy the code in Listing 7-16 into this class.

Listing 7-16. Testing the Core ML Model

```
func testModel()

{

    let model = try? imdbGRU(configuration:
MLModelConfiguration())
```

```swift
    let maxLength = 300
    guard let input_data = try?
MLMultiArray(shape:[NSNumber(value: maxLength),1,1],
dataType:.double) else {

        fatalError("Unexpected runtime error:
input_data")

    }

    input_data[0] = NSNumber(value: 1162)

    input_data[1] = NSNumber(value: 643)

    //padding rest with 0s

    for i in 2..<maxLength {

    input_data[i] = NSNumber(value: 0.0)

    }

    let input = imdbGRUInput(input: input_data,
gru_2_h_in: nil)

    //prediction

    guard let prediction = try?
model?.prediction(input: input) else {

        fatalError("Unexpected runtime error:
prediction")

    }

    print(prediction)
```

```
        //~0.6204907

        print(prediction.output[0])

    }
```

In the preceding code, we create an instance of our model and input data as MLMultiArray shaped [300,1,1]. Core ML models usually work with this type of array called MLMultiArray. We fill this input array with the integer representations of the words "super" and "cool." The rest of the array is filled with zeros (padding). This input array is fed to the model with the prediction function. We print the model's prediction to see if it's as expected.

Open the ContentView file. We will call this method in the onAppear callback of the VStack as shown in Listing 7-17. This will be called when VStack appears on the screen.

Listing 7-17. Call the Model Testing Function

```
var body: some View {

    VStack{

        Text("")

    }.onAppear{

        GRUModel().testModel()

    }

}
```

Now, run the app on a simulator by choosing Product ➤ Run from Xcode's menu or use the cmd+R shortcut. Our expected value is 0.6204907. While debugging, we should see the debugger output as shown in Figure 7-10.

Figure 7-10. *Debugger Output*

Since we checked our model and made sure it works properly, we are ready to use our model in the Xcode project.

Using the Core ML Model in Xcode

We tested the Core ML model and made sure it works correctly. We can check the other details of this model by selecting it in Xcode.

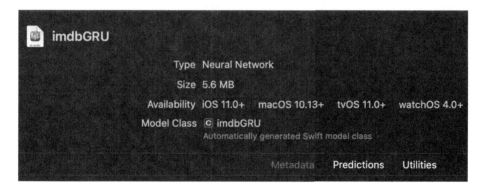

Figure 7-11. *imdbGRU Model in Xcode*

We see the imdbGRU class is automatically generated by Xcode to use this model as shown in Figure 7-11. We will use this class to make a prediction on this model. We will implement the whole project step by step in this chapter. I recommend following the samples and writing the code, but you can also find the completed project here: `https://github.com/ozgurshn/Chapter7-TextClassificationWithGRUModel`.

Create a new file with the name "GRUModel.swift." In this file, we will preprocess the input and make a prediction using the Core ML model.

We will load the word list from the IMDB dataset to an array. You can download the JSON file from this link: `https://storage.googleapis.com/tensorflow/tf-keras-datasets/imdb_word_index.json`. Drag and drop this JSON file into the Xcode project and then copy-paste the code in Listing 7-18.

Listing 7-18. Loading the Word List

```
var wordDictionary: [String: Int] = {

    return try!
JSONDecoder().decode(Dictionary<String, Int>.self,
from: Data(contentsOf:
Bundle.main.url(forResource:"imdb_word_index",
withExtension: "json")!))

}()
```

The first function we will create is the splitToWords function which creates a word list from a string as shown in Listing 7-19. Don't forget to import NaturalLanguage in this class.

Listing 7-19. Splitting Words

```
private func splitToWords(text:String) -> [String]
{
    let lowerCasedText = text.lowercased()

    let tokenizer = NLTokenizer(unit: .word)
```

```
tokenizer.string = lowerCasedText

var tokens = [String]()

tokenizer.enumerateTokens(in:
lowerCasedText.startIndex..<lowerCasedText.endIndex)
{ range, _ in

tokens.append(String(lowerCasedText[range]))

        return true

    }

    return tokens

}
```

In the preceding code, we lowercase the text because our IMDB text representation files contain lowercase words. Then we use NLTokenizer from the Natural Language framework to enumerate words in a given string. We add these words to an array and return that.

The next step is to create the prediction function. Copy-paste the code in Listing 7-20 into the GRUModel class.

Listing 7-20. Prediction

```
func predict(text:String)->String {

    let words = splitToWords(text: text)

    var embedding = [Int]()

    for word in words {

        embedding.append(wordDictionary[word] ?? 0)

    }
```

```
    let model = try? imdbGRU(configuration:
MLModelConfiguration())

    let maxLength = 300

    let maxLengthNumber = NSNumber(value:
maxLength)

    guard let input_data = try?
MLMultiArray(shape:[maxLengthNumber,1,1],
dataType:.double) else {

        fatalError("MLMultiArray error:
input_data")

    }

    for (index,element) in embedding.enumerated()

    {

        input_data[index] = NSNumber(value:
element)

    }

    //padding rest with 0s

    for i in embedding.count..<maxLength {

        input_data[i] = NSNumber(value: 0.0)

    }

    let input =    imdbGRUInput(input: input_data)

    guard let prediction = try?
model?.prediction(input: input) else {
```

```
    fatalError("Prediction error")

}

if prediction.output[0].doubleValue > 0.5

{return "positive"}

else

{return "negative"}

}
```

Here is how the code works:

1. Create a word list from the input string and then
    convert those words to the integer representations
    from wordDictionary.

2. Create the model instance.

3. Create MLMultiArray with size [300,1,1]. We set it to
    300 because we trained our model to take an input
    sized 300.

4. Pad the input data up to 300 with zeros to have a
    fixed size.

5. Create the model input. This class is automatically
    created by Xcode when you drag and drop the
    model into Xcode.

6. Perform the prediction with input data and return
    the result. If the result is higher than 0.5, then the
    result is positive; if it's below 0.5, then the result is
    negative.

Next, we will set up the user interface of our app. Open the ContentView.swift file. Copy-paste the code in Listing 7-21.

Listing 7-21. ContentView

```swift
struct ContentView: View {

    @State var sentiment = ""

    @State var text = "super cool"

    var body: some View {

      VStack{

          TextField("Text", text: $text)

          Button(action: {

              self.sentiment =
GRUModel().predict(text: self.text)

          }){Text("Predict")}

          Text(sentiment)

      }

    }

}
```

In the preceding code, we create two string states to hold prediction result (sentiment) and input text. We use @State, because we want the changes in these variables to be reflected in UI.

In the body of the ContentView, we put the elements in a VStack to organize them vertically. We place a text field to take input from the user, a text view to show the result, and a button to perform the prediction. When the button is tapped, we perform prediction on our machine learning model.

Run the app on a simulator or in live preview mode as shown in Figure 7-12.

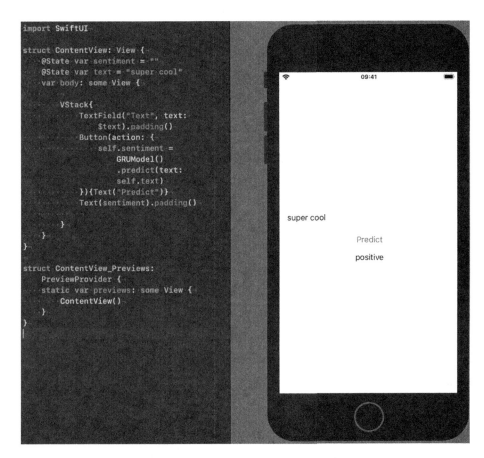

Figure 7-12. *Running the Converted Keras Model in Live Preview*

Tap the Predict button and check the result. Congratulations! You have trained a recurrent neural network model (GRU) with Keras, converted it into Core ML format, and used it in the Xcode project.

Summary

In this chapter, you learned how to use the free Google Colab service to train deep learning models online if you don't have a local Python environment or a good GPU to train your models. We figured out how to use Keras datasets and trained a custom text classification model using the Keras framework. By leveraging the coremltools library, we converted the trained model from Keras to Core ML format and integrated it into the Xcode project. You learned different ways to test your Core ML models using Jupyter Notebook or Xcode. Building a sample application with SwiftUI allowed us to present prediction results to the user easily.

Conclusion

Congratulations! You've completed your journey into building smart apps using machine learning. You've gained the know-how that will hopefully help you in all your future mobile NLP projects.

The NLP world is constantly evolving. We hope that this book has been useful to you as a guide for your first smart application that understands language using NLP techniques.

Index

A

Abstractive text summarization, 122
AlexNet, 11
Algorithms, 8
Apple developer website
    Core ML framework, 36
    ML and Xcode creation, 37
    natural language (*see* Natural
        Language framework)
    speech recognition, 35–36
    Turi creation, 38–39
    vision (*see* Vision framework)
    VisionKit, 26–27

B

Bidirectional Encoder
    Representations from
    Transformers (BERT)
  architectures, 89
  classification layer, 89
  core ML model
    inputs/outputs, 94
    metadata section, 93
    Netron, 96
    tokenization, 95
    Xcode, 93–96

masked LM, 88
next sentence prediction, 90
operating system (iOS)
    BERTInput Class, 99
    bestLogitsIndices
      function, 104
    model instance, 103
    prediction, 103
    project files, 98
    tokenization, 99
    WordID array, 101–102
    word list, 101
principal innovation, 87
question answering
    model, 91–92
SQuAD, 92
SwiftUI application, 97–98
training strategies, 90
user interface (UI)
    attributedText, 106
    question-answering
      App, 111
    search button, 108
    state variables, 106
    SwiftUI app, 105
    TextView creation, 105
    UI elements, 108

C

Core ML framework, 36

D

Deep learning (DL), 10–12
DistilGPT-2 model, 79
Documentation model, 87
    BERT (*see* Bidirectional Encoder
        Representations from
        Transformers (BERT))

E, F

Error function, 8
Extractive summarization, 121

G, H

Gated Recurrent Unit (GRU), 144
Generative Pretrained Transformer
    (GPT)
    built-in OCR model, 71
    coremltools, 70
    DistilGPT-2 model, 71
    text prediction, 70
    transformation, 69

I

ImageNet dataset, 10–12
Iteration/epoch data, 8

J

Jupyter notebook
    Core ML model, 149
    input size error, 152
    model specification, 151
    output, 153
    prediction, 152
    print model specs, 150
    virtual environment, 149

K, L

Keras models
    classification model
        Colab cell, 138
        compilation method,
          145–146
        core ML format, 147
        creation, 144
        distribution graph, 142
        IMDB dataset, 140–141
        libraries, 138–139
        model's summarization, 145
        pad sequences, 143
        sequential class, 144
        training results, 146
        word count distribution, 142
        word representations, 140
    Colab, 138
    deep learning libraries, 137
    testing-core ML model, 147–157
    Xcode model, 157–163

M

Machine learning (ML)
  AI models, 1
  categories, 4
  cutting-edge tools, 2
  DL (*see* Deep learning (DL))
  history, 1
  positive/negative emails, 3
  prediction, 4
  smart apps, 2
  supervised learning, 5–6
  training model, 3
  unsupervised learning, 6–9
macOS playground
  accuracy, 49
  auto-generated class code, 53
  check training metrics, 49
  classifier model, 53
  core ML model, 50
  CreateML/foundation, 43–44
  error handling, 47
  evaluation, 49
  MLModel project, 51
  MLTextClassifier, 47
  model details, 52
  parsing options, 46
  playground settings, 44
  prediction, 50
  SpamClassifier class, 52
  spam SMS classifier app, 56–57
  splits data, 48
  SwiftUI, 54

  templates, 43
  text classification, 46
  training output, 48
  URL object, 45

N, O, P, Q

Natural language processing (NLP)
  advantages, 12
  framework models
    enumerating words, 28
    language identification, 27
    NLEmbedding, 34–35
    part-of-speech tagging,
      30–31
    people, places/organizations,
      32–34
    tokenization, 29–30
    word tagging, 30
  language modeling, 13
  mathematical
    calculations, 13–14
  neural network–based
    methods, 12
  N-grams, 13
  objective, 12
  pretrained language models, 14
  sequence-to-sequence
    (Seq2Seq), 14
  word embedding, 13
Next Sentence Prediction (NSP), 90
NLEmbedding, 34–35
NLTagger, 30–31

R

Recurrent neural
    network (RNN), 143

S

Spam classification
  create ML, 41
  create ML app
    CSV/text file creation, 58–59
    project templates, 57–58
    static and dynamic
      embedding, 61
    text files, 60
    training data panel, 60
    training status/accuracy, 61
  entities, 42
  SMS collection dataset, 43
  text classification, 42
  Turi creation
    bag-of-words
      representation, 65
    iPython, 63
    meaning, 62
    setup, 62–63
    text classifier, 64–67
    virtual environment, 63
Speech framework, 35–36
Speech recognition/framework
  audio transcription, 113–115
  ContentView struct, 117
  descriptions, 112
  permission request, 113

  processing app, 117
  speak button, 116
  text-to-speech function, 117–118
  transcription permission, 112
Stanford Question Answering
    Dataset (SQuAD), 92
Summarization techniques, 121
  abstractive, 122
  button action, 134
  ContentView file, 124–125
  extractive, 121
  function, 132
  natural language framework, 126
  project creation, 123
  SentenceAndRank, 126
  splitting function, 129
  stop words declaration, 126–128
  SwiftUI preview testing, 125
  text editor, 134
  word frequencies, 130–132
Supervised learning, 5–6

T

Testing-core ML model
  Colab environment, 147–149
  integer representations, 148
  Jupyter notebook, 149–154
  prediction, 148
  word embedding, 148
  Xcode, 154–157
Text classification
  macOS playground, 43–57

sentiment analysis, 41

spam (*see* Spam classification)

Text generation models

AI models

Anne Karenina, 85

decoding strategies, 80

generation function, 82–83

GPT files, 78

handling tap gesture, 83

metadata, 78

prediction function, 80–81

generative pertained

transformer, 69–72

OCR functions

captureOutput function, 74

recognizeTextHandler

function, 76

scanning resources, 72

showString method, 76

starter project, 72–73

text recognition request,

74–77

viewDidLoad function, 76

views and GPT folders, 73

VisionViewController

functions, 74

Text-to-speech function, 117–118

U

Unsupervised learning, 7–9

V, W

Vision framework

face/body detection, 18–19

horizon detection, 25

image analysis capabilities

classification, 20

comparison, 22

ImageRequestHandler, 20

knownClassifications

method, 19

mathematical

representation, 21

meaning, 19

ML capabilities, 17

object recognition, 25

saliency analysis, 25

text detection and

recognition, 22–24

VisionKit, 26–27

X, Y, Z

Xcode model

ContentView file, 162

debugger output, 157

drag and drop model, 154

imdbGRU model, 157

MLMultiArray, 156

model testing

function, 156

prediction function, 159–161

preview mode, 163

splitting words, 158

testing, 154–155

word list loading, 158

working process, 161

Printed in the United States
By Bookmasters